CHRISTMAS
1984

Decorating & Craft Ideas®

for Christmas 1984

BY
SHELLEY STEWART
JO VOCE

OXMOOR
HOUSE®

Decorating & Craft Ideas® is a federally registered
trademark of Southern Living, Inc.

ISSN: 0742-8154
ISBN: 0-8487-0635-8
Manufactured in the United States of America
First Printing

CONTENTS

INTRODUCTION

INTRODUCTION

If you are a woman who enjoys being involved, and who adds a creative touch to everything you do, then you know that planning for Christmas can be almost as much fun as the day itself. Spend a little time getting organized so that those last few weeks of the year will be free for you to participate in all the seasonal activities that your family enjoys. Begin now— and let this big book of ideas be your guide. Use the easy-to-follow instructions to make exciting decorations and crafts like those shown, or let these be a starting point for your own imagination!

All projects are photographed in full color, in settings much like your own home, which may give you some good ideas for displaying the items you make. Instructions are written in clear language, with a list of necessary materials written in bolder type so that you may be sure you have everything you need before you begin. Full-size patterns for most projects appear in the back of the book, complete with color keys.

WELCOME THE SEASON is filled with easy and inexpensive ideas for decorating your home both inside and out. There are wreaths and garlands, mantels and mailboxes, trees and trimmings, plus a number of "free" ideas using household items that any craftswoman probably has on hand.

HANDMADE WITH LOVE offers a host of ideas for gifts and Christmas crafts, each done in one of the most popular craft techniques, such as candlewicking, embroidery, soft sculpture, or painting on wood. There are projects for any level of skill too; many that appear complicated are surprisingly simple!

YOUR CHRISTMAS KITCHEN is packed with some of the most delicious recipes you'll ever serve to your family and friends. There are foods to make ahead for gifts, fragrant holiday breads, pies, cakes and cookies, and enough recipes for special occasions to let you entertain to your heart's content.

The time is now, the book is here—so use it, and let 1984 be the one that you remember in the years to come as your Merriest Christmas ever!

WHEN COMPANY COMES

Sometimes a dining room table just can't be stretched enough to accommodate all of your guests; yet you certainly don't want anyone to feel slighted by being seated at an ordinary card table. If you have ever had such a problem, this card table cover may be the solution.

Made to cover a standard-sized 30" table, this very practical cloth is trimmed with enormous snap-on bows and bright grosgrain ribbon. Turn the cloth over, and you have a solid color to use, minus bows, throughout the year. Extra fabric is made into matching covers for the backs of your chairs, which gives the grouping a tailored appearance.

To decorate the top of the table, a potted plant is wrapped with two napkins, turned at angles to each other and gathered with a ribbon around the pot. Tiny ribbon bows are placed like blossoms on the leaves—a touch that children especially will appreciate. Napkins are folded and tied with ribbon to match the cloth.

YOU WILL NEED (for card table cover):
3¼ yds. (45"-wide) double-faced
   quilted fabric
thread to match ribbon *and* wrong
   side of fabric
5⅔ yds. (⅝"-wide) grosgrain ribbon
6 yds. (1½"-wide) grosgrain ribbon
4 Velcro® fasteners
1⅛ yds. (60"-wide) red fabric (for bows)

Prewash and iron all ribbon before beginning. Thread machine with thread to match wrong side of fabric. Cut quilted fabric to size: cut one piece 45" x 56"; then cut two strips 6" x 56". (You will have a large amount of fabric remaining—use this for chair covers or the quilted casserole carrier shown on page 63.)

Sew one strip to 56"-long side of large piece with *wrong* sides together, using a ½" seam. Press seam allowance toward large piece. Trim away all but ¼" on bottom seam allowance, letting top layer fold over to

cover. Attach strip to other side in same manner and trim. Turn up ½" around all edges, toward right side, stitching ¼" from edge as you go. (Rough edges will be hidden later with ribbon.)

Change thread in machine so that top-stitching will match ribbon, leaving previous color in bobbin. Topstitch 56" of ⅝"-wide ribbon to each side to cover seam where strip is joined. Topstitch two more 56"-long pieces of ⅝"-wide ribbon to remaining sides of cover, placing them same distance away from edge as those ribbons covering seams. (Ribbons will cross near corner.)

Leaving about ¼" of fabric showing as a border, topstitch a band of 1½"-wide ribbon around all 4 sides, mitering corners. Top-stitch mitered corners. (Ribbon will now hide all rough edges.) If you are adding bows, find center point of narrow ribbon on each side, marking with a pin. Sew a Velcro® fastener on each mark.

BOWS: Cut four strips (10" x 60") from red fabric. Fold each strip lengthwise with right sides facing and sew around edges, leaving an opening for turning. Turn, blindstitch opening closed, and press.

Cut one strip 10" x 30"; seam down long side with right sides facing. Turn, press, and cut into 4 equal sections. To make each section, turn raw edges in ½" and tack ends together to form a ring. Sew matching Velcro® fastener over seam line. Cross ends of long strip to make a bow shape and pull ring over one loop and one end to hold in place. Repeat for other bows.

YOU WILL NEED (for 4 chair covers):
½ yd. (45"-wide) double-faced quilted fabric (or fabric remaining from table cover)
10 yds. (⅝"-wide) grosgrain ribbon
thread to match ribbon *and* wrong side of fabric

These covers fit over the back of most ladderback chairs or folding card table chairs. If your chairs are wider than average, add an extra 8" to each ribbon used to make the ties (for a total of 1¾ yards of extra ribbon).

From quilted fabric, cut four 11" x 16" pieces. Turn up ½" around all edges, toward right side, stitching ¼" from edge as you go. Topstitch ⅝" ribbon (14"-long) to hide raw edges on long sides. Topstitch two ribbons (each 36"-long or longer) to remaining sides, leaving equal amounts of ribbon free on ends. Fold cover over back of chair, cross ribbons, and tie a bow at each side.

NAPKIN FOLD: Fold napkin once diagonally (figure 1). Fold left and right corners toward center (figure 2). Roll left and right edges toward center (figure 3). Hold in place and tie with a ribbon bow.★

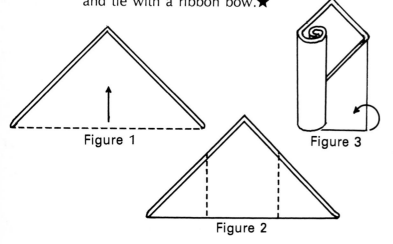

Figure 1

Figure 2

Figure 3

GOLDEN NUT TREE

Besides being lovely to look at, this tree made of golden-toned fruits and nuts has an added advantage—with proper storage between seasons, it will last for years and years. Not many decorations are so durable. After Christmas, wrap the tree in tissue and place it in a spot that is cool and dry.

The basic construction is simple—a plastic foam shape is covered with mastic; then the fruits and nuts are pressed on. The mastic hardens, leaving the "ornaments" permanently implanted. If a nut should fall off later, another can be put in its place with a dab of glue.

Display the tree with a few branches of greenery, some fruits, and nuts at the base for an attractive, old-fashioned arrangement.

YOU WILL NEED:
plastic foam cone
tile mastic (brown)
assorted nuts
small pine cone
lacquered artificial fruits
small plastic holly leaves
small can or dish (for base)
spray paint (gold metallic)
spray varnish (glossy)

Using an old putty knife or a plastic knife that you don't mind discarding, spread a layer of mastic on the plastic cone. (You may find it easiest to work on one side at a time.) Allow the mastic to dry until it is "tacky"; then press the nuts on, beginning at the bottom and working upward. Top the tree with a small pine cone. Fill in large spaces between the nuts with small lacquered fruits and plastic holly leaves. Allow to dry.

Meanwhile, spray whatever you have chosen for the base with gold metallic paint. When the paint dries, place a bit of mastic on the top of the base and attach the base to the cone. When completely dry, spray the tree with several coats of glossy varnish, allowing it to dry between coats.★

4

WINTER WONDERLAND

Plump little snowmen play hide-and-seek in a forest of evergreens made from painted wood. Although shown as a centerpiece, the arrangement might also be used on a mantel, a buffet, or a coffee table. Vary it from year to year by adding a sprinkling of artificial snow, some drifts of angel hair, loops of curly ribbon, or clippings of greenery at the base of the trees. If you like, make a matching snowman box to fill with candies.

YOU WILL NEED:
patterns on pages 130 and 131
scraps of white pine shelving (¾"-thick)
band saw or jigsaw
lath strips (for box only)
sandpaper
sealer
white household glue, metal brads, and
    wood putty (for box only)
liquid acrylic paints
water-based varnish

The number of trees and snowmen is determined by how large you want the arrangement to be (eleven trees of varying sizes are shown in photograph). Transfer patterns for trees and snowmen to wood, with grain of wood running from top to bottom. Cut all figures with saw; then sand smooth and apply a coat of sealer.

Paint front, back, and edges of all pieces. Paint trees with acrylic paints on a medium brush, using green shaded with blue. When dry, dip wrong end of a small brush into white paint and make dots for snowflakes.

To make snowman, paint face and body with white shaded with gray. Stipple with shades of green to make wreath and add dots of red for berries. Paint hat, scarf, mittens, bow, and nose with red, shading slightly if desired. Paint hair with a mixture of gold and brown; then add facial features with black. Dot with white to make snowflakes on red areas. Apply a coat of water-based varnish.

SNOWMAN BOX: Follow general directions for cutting given above, but cut four sides of box using same pattern. Before painting, glue sides of box together (see pattern), securing with tiny brads at corners. Countersink brads and fill holes with wood putty. Cut lath strips to width of box and tack to bottom with brads.

Transfer pattern for snowman to each side of box, and paint as directed above (see photograph). Paint background and inside of box with white. Allow paint to dry and coat with varnish for protection.★

FANCIFUL PYRAMIDS

Of all the traditional forms of decorating handed down from colonial times, none is more impressive than the towering fruit pyramid. Originally used only in homes of the very wealthy, they were made predominantly of local apples and green leaves, with the occasional added luxury of an imported pineapple. Because they are large and tend to dominate smaller accessories, they are best used as centerpieces or buffet decorations—especially at parties, where they are sure to cause admiring comments.

When making a pyramid, it is important to start with a sturdy base, as the finished decoration will be quite heavy. If possible, make the pyramid where it will be used, to avoid having to carry it. Colonial women started with a base of three firm cabbages in graduated sizes, flattened at the bottom and held together by knitting needles or skewers. This idea is still practical. You might also use one of the wooden bases with protruding metal spikes (available from many museum shops or specialty stores) or a firm plastic foam

8

cone attached to a heavy platter with florist's clay. Unless you are using the wood and metal base, you will need to have some wooden florist's picks to attach the fruit. (Do not eat fruit which has been punctured by these picks—the dyes in some picks are poisonous.) Toothpicks are not usually strong enough to hold the fruits, but sections of bamboo skewers might serve as well, and the fruit could then be eaten.

Today, the abundance of fresh fruits seen in supermarkets opens up a variety of possibilities for making pyramids. The choices of fruits are many, depending upon your own preference and the length of time that the arrangement must last. Choose firm, slightly under-ripe fruits when possible; lemons, limes, oranges or baking apples tend to last longest, while bananas are best not used at all. For special occasions, when one glorious night is all that matters, you might even add some cascading clusters of grapes or fresh flowers. Polish the fruit with a soft cloth before inserting the picks.

Begin at the bottom with a layer of greenery to cover the base. Work around the form when adding fruits, remembering that empty spaces between may be filled with greenery. Continue toward the top, keeping the weight evenly balanced. Fill in the gaps with short pieces of boxwood, cedar, pittosporum, or

any other long-lasting evergreens, holding them in place with floral pins if necessary. (Remember that if you intend to eat the fruit, the greenery also must be non-poisonous.)

The two examples shown here, both impressive, indicate just how much a pyramid may vary. The one with the red delicious apples is the more traditional because it uses only one type of fruit. Built on a wooden form set on a metal platter, it has an abundance of flat cedar and boxwood greenery used as filler. Placed on a pine chest that serves as a coffee table, it is definitely in keeping with the warm and friendly character of the room.

A reverence for tradition, coupled with a willingness to try new ideas, resulted in the exuberant fruit and flower pyramid encircled by vines. Two types of apples, oranges, lemons, limes, and a pineapple add their colors, with the surprising addition of cut limes and tender white narcissus blossoms. The whole arrangement rests on a base of broad green magnolia leaves. Colorful plaid napkins are wrapped with a length of ribbon, and each guest receives a gift of fragrant flowers tucked inside.★

NEW-FASHIONED YO-YOS

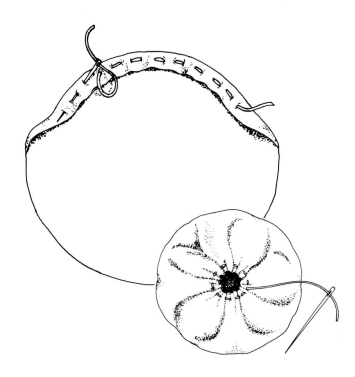

If Grandma could see this wreath, she would pull out her scrap bag and start making more yo-yos! Gathered like the yo-yos seen in prized antique coverlets, these are sewn onto a wreath form trimmed with eyelet and a bow. Others are stitched together to make yards of garland to swag across the mantel or tree. The jar toppers use only two yo-yos each but add holiday color to your homemade goodies.

YOU WILL NEED (for one wreath):
corrugated cardboard (13" x 13" square)
½ yd. solid green fabric
glue stick
⅜ yd. each of 3 green print fabrics
¼ yd. red print (for berries)
⅜ yd. red print (for berries and bow)
iron-on interfacing (4" x 36")
40" (2"-wide) pregathered eyelet or lace
small drapery ring

WREATH: Cut a 12" circle from cardboard; cut a 5"-wide center opening to make a wreath form.

Place wreath form on solid green fabric and trace around outline two separate times. Cut wreaths, adding ½" seam allowance to inner edge of both, and ½" to outer edge of one wreath only.

With right sides of wreaths facing, stitch around inner circle. Clip around curve every ½", turn, and press. Slip over cardboard form. Rub glue stick around outer edge of cardboard on back side. Press edge of smaller fabric circle onto glue to hold. Pull larger circle over edge, turn under narrow hem, and pin to cover raw edge. Slipstitch to back.

To make patterns for yo-yos, cut three circles (4½"-, 3¾"-, and 2¾"-wide). Using green print fabrics and scraps of solid green, cut circles according to patterns. (In all, you will need about 20 large, 20 medium, and 12 small sizes.) Use small pattern to cut circles from two red prints. (You will need about 20 of these for berries.)

Hem around each circle by turning under ¼" and sewing with a running stitch (see diagrams). Pull thread to gather. Before knotting, flatten circle and fasten with a few stitches through center.

To make bow, cut strip (8" x 36") from red fabric. Fold in half lengthwise with wrong sides together and press crease. Cut strip of iron-on interfacing (4" x 36"), insert in red fabric, and press to bond to one side. Fold with *right* sides together; stitch long edge and across both ends at a slight angle, using a ¼" seam and leaving an opening for turning. Turn and press. Tie into bow.

Whipstitch eyelet ruffle to back of wreath. Arrange yo-yos to cover front, beginning with large size around outer edge and filling in with smaller ones, randomly spaced to cover background fabric. (Stick a straight pin through each to hold.) Sew in place like a button, going through both yo-yo and cardboard with a sharp needle and doubled thread. Attach bow in the same manner and tack on a small drapery ring for hanging.

GARLAND: Using extra scraps of fabrics used in wreath, make a variety of yo-yos according to directions given above. Sew yo-yos end to end with whipstitches, knotting thread each time. Continue until garland is as long as desired.

JAR TOPPER: Paint ring of jar with any lead-free enamel paint. Cut circle of fabric to size of jar lid, allowing an extra ½" all around. Sew narrow pregathered eyelet around circle to cover raw edge. Center medium and small yo-yo on circle, taking a few stitches through all layers to hold. Place over lid of jar and screw ring on top.★

BURLAP & BEARS

Bears, bears, bears! If you have loved these cuddly creatures since you were a child yourself, why not delight your own children by letting your holiday decorations be based on bears?

Sew the burlap tree skirt with its design of tumbling bears; then use the extra burlap to make little sacks to fill with special treats. Continue the theme with a whole troupe of movable bears made from brown paper grocery bags—your child can help with these! Make a few extra bears to march across your window or mantel, or to use as package ties.

YOU WILL NEED (to make tree skirt):
pattern on page 138
1 yd. natural burlap
1 yd. muslin (for lining)
brown paper
marking pencil
½ yd. small plaid woven fabric
½ yd. iron-on interfacing
thread to contrast
1⅔ yds. (45"-wide) green fabric (for ruffle)
2 packages bias seam binding
7 (½"-wide) black buttons

Cut a 36"-wide circle from both burlap and muslin. Pin together; then cut a 6" circle in the middle, also cutting a line from circle to edge of skirt. Baste by hand to outline edges and to divide skirt into six sections, using contrasting thread. (This step keeps fabrics from slipping; the stitches will be removed.)

Transfer pattern pieces to brown paper; cut 2 legs, 2 arms and 1 body. Insert a paper clasp or pin through points marked with an "X" so that pieces are attached but can move.

Move paper bear around until you are pleased with pose; then trace outline of paper onto right side of interfacing. (Bears will face in opposite direction on finished tree skirt.) Cut around outline, fuse to plaid fabric, and trim plaid fabric to same outline. Repeat steps to make seven 2-layer bears.

Disassemble paper bear. Place individual pieces on right side of plaid fabric and mark any lines, such as tummy or top of leg, that need to be outlined. Pin plaid bears to burlap, spacing them as desired. Hand baste about ¼" from edge. Appliqué, using a ⅛"-wide, closely spaced zigzag stitch.

To make ruffle, tear six (10"-wide) strips across the width of green fabric. Seam end to end with right sides together; fold in half lengthwise, pressing as you go. Gather ruffle to fit around tree skirt and sew together (skirt edge should barely overlap gathered stitching on ruffle).

Cover cut straight edges and inner circle with seam binding and sew. Cover raw outer edge of tree skirt with more seam binding, stitching close to both sides of binding. Sew eyes on bears. Remove basting threads.

BURLAP BAG ORNAMENTS: For each ornament, cut a piece of burlap 4½" x 13". Fold end to end; then sew side seams. Turn right sides out and pull threads to ravel top. Fold edge down and tack yarn or ribbon across top to act as hanger. Fill with assorted treats or small toys.

YOU WILL NEED (to make bear ornament):
pattern on page 138
brown grocery bag
Stitch Witchery® fusible fabric bond
black marking pen
scraps of red fabric
2 brass paper clasps

Each ornament is made of stiffened brown paper grocery bags. To stiffen, make a "sandwich" from two smooth layers of paper with a layer of Stitch Witchery® fusible fabric bond between; press to join all layers. Cut 2 legs, 2 arms, and 1 body according to pattern. Stick a straight pin through all points marked "X" on pattern to mark place. Draw details on bears with black marking pen.

Cut 2 vests from red fabric and 2 from Stitch Witchery® for each bear. Cut 2 bows from each fabric for girl bears only. Press to bond vest (and bow) to body on each side.

Using pin holes as your guide, enlarge holes enough to insert a brass paper clasp. Attach legs and arms to body. Glue a loop for hanging at top if desired.★

TINY TREASURE

Standing less than two inches tall, this roly-poly peasant may well be the tiniest decoration on your tree. Her jolly face and plump little body are made with wooden beads and cotton-stuffed fabric circles.

If you prefer to use her as jewelry for a young lady in your family, just sew a small gold ring to the top of her head and hang from a ribbon to make a necklace. Or tack a small brass safety pin to her back to make a holiday lapel pin.

YOU WILL NEED:
one (14 mm.) wooden bead (for head)
two (8 mm.) wooden beads (for hands)
acrylic paint (flesh, red, black, pink)
scraps of holiday-print fabrics and satin
quilting thread
cotton balls
5" (½"-wide) double-edged lace
pipecleaner
white household glue

Paint all beads with flesh-color; then paint a face on the large bead and set aside. To make the base, cut a 2½"-diameter circle from satin and baste by hand about ¼" from the edge. Draw up the thread to form a pouch, stuff with cotton, and pull tight to close. Knot and clip the thread.

Begin the torso in the same way, using a 1¾"-diameter circle of print fabric. Stuff and close, *not* clipping the thread. Place the gathered sides of the base and torso together and sew around the middle to hold. Knot the thread, still not cutting. Baste down the middle of the lace and gather around the waist (the spot where the ends of the lace overlap is the back). Tie off the thread.

From a different print fabric, cut a 1½" x 1¾" sleeve. (If you are making a number of ornaments at one time, cut a strip of fabric 1½" wide and as long as you choose.) Fold the sleeve (or strip) with right sides together, stitch the long edge with a ¼" seam, trim the seam, and turn right side out. (Cut off

sections 1¾" long to make sleeves if using the longer strip.)

Turn under ¼" at each end of the sleeve and insert a 1¾" piece of pipecleaner for arms. Glue on the small beads for hands. Bend the sleeve over the torso, checking first to see where the back is. Tack the sleeve at the middle; then sew on the head, face forward, so that the thread comes down the back of the head. Take several stitches through the back before clipping.

Cut a 2" square of fabric for the shawl. Fold diagonally with right sides together and sew a ¼" seam on two sides, leaving an opening for turning. Turn and press. Dab glue on the back of the head, center the shawl, and cross the corners in front. Tack with thread to hold.★

CRISP PLAID PLACEMATS

Set a fine holiday table with these colorful plaid mats made like miniature canvas floorcloths. No painting whatsoever is involved in making the clean, straight lines. What is the secret? You use a ruler and permanent marking pens!

The instant centerpiece is another easy idea. Instead of trying to find a suitable container for an expensive arrangement, just gift wrap the bottom of several small boxes, place glasses of water inside, and fill with clippings of pine or other greenery.

YOU WILL NEED (for 4 mats):
1⅛ yds. (48"-wide) primed canvas
L-shaped ruler or a yardstick
masking tape
permanent marking pens (El Marko® by
 Flair or Carter's Marks-A-Lot®—red,
 green, yellow, blue)
acrylic spray
white household glue
1⅛ yds. dark green felt
Spray Mount® adhesive

NOTE: It is essential to test your acrylic spray in combination with your markers. Before making the mats, make a test strip of all four colors of marker on a scrap of primed canvas. Spray with acrylic three times, drying between coats. If your colors bleed, choose another brand of acrylic spray or make sure you are using the proper markers.

Steam press wrong side of canvas if necessary to remove wrinkles. Cut four pieces (20" x 24") from canvas. In center of each mat, measure and pencil a rectangle 7½" x 12", being careful that corners are square. Place masking tape along *inside* edges of this rectangle. Tape a piece of paper to cover center area and prevent smudges. Measure exactly 2¼" outside this rectangle and mark again to make a second rectangle (it should measure 12" x 16½"). Place masking tape on *outside* edge of this larger rectangle.

Beginning at top right corner just inside larger rectangle, measure 1½" and place a dot at that spot with a pencil. Continue around rectangle, making a dot every 1½".

Red: Beginning at bottom left corner, place ruler so that it crosses first dots on two adjacent sides. Draw along edge of ruler with broad side of red marker. Continue drawing lines with red, moving up one dot on each side every time, until you reach opposite corner. (Do not draw across paper in center. You should have parallel lines of red between lines of tape.)

Turn mat so that a narrow edge is toward you. Beginning at bottom left corner again, draw a red line from dot to dot as you did before, working your way to opposite corner.

(Pattern will look like a windowpane check with a white square in the middle.)

Green: Turn mat one-quarter turn again. Holding a ruler on top edge of red line, draw another line with broad side of green marker. Repeat steps, as you did with red marker, so that you end with a windowpane check of red and green.

Yellow: Yellow markers sometimes smear even though they are permanent. Do not cross red or green lines with yellow—work only in white squares. Still using your ruler for accuracy, make a cross in center of all white squares (see photograph above).

Blue: The pattern now changes. Beginning at bottom left again, place ruler on bottom of yellow marks and draw a line with narrow side of blue marker. Work as before, toward top right corner. Turn mat one-quarter turn and repeat from bottom left, drawing lines with blue under yellow lines until you reach top right. This completes plaid pattern.

Remove tape and paper. Edges of plaid may have bled a little beneath tape. To cover, place ruler on outside edge of larger rectangle; then outline each side with broad side of green marker. Repeat to make a border on inside edge of smaller rectangle.

Tack edges of canvas to something flat, such as plywood or cardboard. Spray lightly with acrylic spray, allow to dry, and repeat two more times for a total of three coats.

Fold edges toward back, leaving a ½"-wide white border outside green border. Do *not* cut along fold line; cut ½" outside of fold line. Miter corners and glue edges to back. Cut felt to size of mat. Trim ¼" from edge all around and center on back of mat.

Fold felt so that only half shows; spray adhesive on underside of felt as well as back of half of canvas. Press with fingers to adhere; then repeat for other half.

To clean mats, wipe fronts with a damp cloth. Do not submerge in water.★

FIESTA TIME!

Vibrant with the colors of Old Mexico, this large *Ojo de Dios* (Eye-of-God) is perfectly suited to your *Feliz Navidad* celebrations. Adapted from a very ancient Indian custom, Eyes-of-God were originally made by fathers for their children. Each rhomboid shape counted for a year of the child's life, and the deity could "look" through the center and see the child, thereby offering him protection from harm. This one is made for decoration only, and is a symbol of the holiday spirit.

To accompany the Eye-of-God, make some stylized sun-faced ornaments with decoratively twisted edges. The hot pinks, yellows, and oranges of the ornaments are bright against the tree and provide a nice change from the more typical red and green color scheme.

EYE-OF-GOD: This free-standing decoration is large, 18"-wide and 24"-high, which makes it an ideal size for a buffet or an entrance hall table. To make a larger or smaller version, just change the dimensions of the dowels.

Look at figure 1 to see how the yarn is wrapped over and under the dowels to hold them together. Wrap the yarn once around each dowel as you move from one to the next (a ridge will form on the back side). Change colors of yarn or the direction in which you wrap to form different patterns, making sure that both sides are symmetrical.

This decoration is constructed mainly from ⅛"-diameter dowels, with a ¼"-diameter dowel (24"-long) used for the vertical center piece. You will need a total of 5½ feet of ⅛" dowel and 2 feet of ¼" dowel. Cut the ⅛" dowel as follows: one 18" length, two 10" lengths, three 7" lengths, and two 4" lengths. Consult the diagrams as you work.

Form a cross from the 24"- and 18"-long pieces, wrapping with yarn (figure 2). Attach two 10"-long pieces vertically on ends of horizontal dowel, again wrapping. Add two 7" pieces at top of center dowel; then add

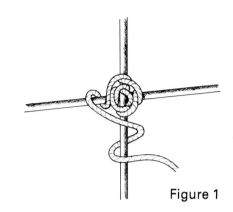

Figure 1

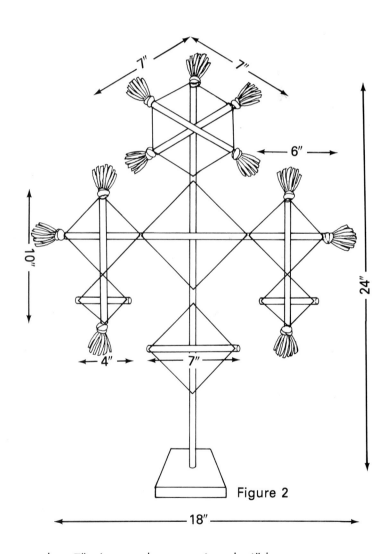

Figure 2

other 7" piece at bottom. Attach 4"-long pieces to bottom of vertical side pieces. Add tassels to exposed ends of dowels. Insert finished decoration into a stand made by drilling a ¼" hole in a block of wood.★

19

TASSELS: Make each tassel by wrapping yarn seven or eight times around a 2"-wide piece of cardboard. Tie with another piece of yarn at one side; then cut all loops at the other side. Wrap more yarn tightly around the whole bunch about ½" below where it is tied (see diagram above).

Use tassels individually as ornaments or join several with multi-colored lengths of yarn to form a garland for your tree.

YARN ORNAMENTS: Another way of making colorful yarn ornaments is simply to run a line of white household glue around a plastic foam ball, coiling a double or triple strand of yarn around to follow the glue. Be careful not to change the position of the colors as you work. Add a loop at the top for hanging.

SUN-FACE ORNAMENTS: Each ornament is made from the slightly curved bottom of an aluminum soft drink can. Cut the bottom off with kitchen shears, leaving from ½" to 1" of the straight sides attached. Clip this side at regular intervals in either a straight or a slanted pattern. Apply a coat of high-gloss enamel paint to cover both sides and all cut edges; allow to dry.

Using needle-nosed pliers, gently twist each cut section to form a curled or bent shape. Bend each section the same way or alternate the pattern, as long as you are consistent. Touch up any paint that has chipped off; then add a painted face in a contrasting color.★

HOLIDAY SLIPCOVERS

Sometimes it is fun to do something completely unexpected—surprise your family by transforming everyday furniture into furniture fit for the season with holiday slipcovers! The bright colors of Christmas-print fabrics are a light-hearted contrast to most year-round upholstery.

Because the covers are only temporary, there is no need for elaborate workmanship—the fabric may be stretched around the cushions of sofas and chairs, secured by masking tape on the underside. (If the tape does not touch the cushion itself, only the new fabric, it should in no way damage your furniture.)

If your cushions are wider than the fabric, seam two sections together before wrapping the furniture. Tuck the extra fabric on the sides under the cushion, just as you would if you were making a bed.

Bolster pillows in a complimentary fabric are an attractive accent to the room. This is the biggest surprise of all. They are made from big, fluffy towels that have been folded lengthwise, rolled up and pinned, then wrapped with more fabric and tied at the ends with ribbon (see diagrams).★

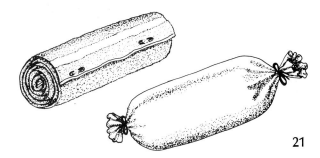

COLLECTIONS ON MANTELS

As the focal point for the whole room, a mantel is also the first place most people think of decorating. The decorations should be simple to make, really spectacular, and above all, not too close to the fire!

These two mantels are ideal examples of the easiest way to decorate—using a collection you already have, supplemented by greenery, with extra glow added by candles.

A lifetime collection of angels is displayed on one mantel—angels of every description in brass and copper—some molded, some made of wire, all very pretty. (The nice thing about a collection is that it seems to grow automatically. Once your friends know what you are collecting, they are eager to add to it each time an occasion calls for a little gift!)

The angels are arranged across the full length of the mantel, together with brass candlesticks and a few musical instruments. Short lengths of evergreen branches are placed behind and around the base of the angels; then bright red candles are tucked into all of the candlesticks. Even when the candles are not lit, the effect of the red against the green and bright metal is lovely. The diversity of the collection almost seems to say "Come over and look."

Another collection of brass candlesticks, without the angels, decorates the second mantel. Any candlesticks would create much the same effect, even if they were made of different materials. The important element is the arrangement. Whether the composition is symmetrical or asymmetrical, it is usually most pleasing if you vary the heights by having different lengths of candles, even if the holders are all the same height. Rich-colored candles are definitely in order at Christmas, especially if the wall above is light.

Again, greenery works its wonders by adding height for good balance and filling in the empty space between candlesticks. A solitary deer (the first piece in a new collection?) stands near the center to give focus to the arrangement.★

PINECONES IN FANCY DRESS

Draped with garlands of beads that look like plump cranberries, the coniferous evergreen tree is a natural setting for these ornaments made from cones. The spruce and mugho pine cones act as bases for an assortment of trimmings, which might be varied to suit your taste.

Tiny alder or hemlock cones, lacquered red berries, a bright red cardinal, and a small, fuzzy bear are the central elements that top these cones. Sprigs of preserved or plastic cedar are tucked underneath, and puffy loops of ribbon add a final accent. (The directions for making never-fail bows are given on page 60.)

An electric glue gun is most practical for making any ornament that has separate parts attached. If you do not have one of these handy tools, use a quick-setting white household glue, anchoring the parts with pins.★

A WELCOME FOR FRIENDS

This unusual centerpiece does double duty as both a table decoration and a novel way of dispensing gifts to your guests. Wrap tiny gift packages in foil and tie with shiny gold ribbons; then pile them high in the top of an "epergne" made of two stacked wooden salad bowls. Place a small dish between the two bowls to create more height before tucking in sprigs of greenery and berries. When it is time for guests to leave, let each of them choose one of the gifts.

The runner is made from a narrow length of green felt. Cut each end into shape, as shown, and stitch a row of fancy braid about one inch from the edge, following the contours of the runner.★

THOSE SPECIAL MEMORIES

Sharp memories disappear over the years to be replaced by hazy impressions, yet sometimes a simple object brought into view can crystallize those images of so long ago and make them seem like only yesterday.

What time of year could be more appropriate for creating your own "memory" cabinet—filled with all those irreplaceable items valuable only to you? Your daughter's first tea set or your son's tiny cowboy boots...or the tinsel angel that you and your husband tenderly placed atop your first tree. These things are important and should receive notice, as symbols of important times in your family's life together.

Choose a small cabinet, or a shelf in a bookcase, or even a tabletop in a corner of the room. Arrange your treasures and add a few trimmings of greenery or candles. When the season is over, pack them up for another year, but plan on letting this display be a part of every Christmas in the future.★

"BUSTER BEAR" COLLAGE

Your child would be delighted if you hung this winsome bear collage in his room. Although made of fabric, the collage requires no sewing—each shape is sprayed with adhesive and smoothed onto the background. The "spray and press" technique is so easy that you will enjoy making these collages as gifts. Vary your designs by adapting the patterns you find in children's coloring books.

YOU WILL NEED:
patterns on pages 128 and 129
matboard (12" x 15")
scraps of mini-print fabrics
Spray Mount® adhesive
white household glue
small amount embroidery floss
felt-tipped marker (black finepoint)
purchased frame with mat cut to size

Transfer patterns to fabrics, using colors suggested by the photograph or others that you have on hand. Press fabric. Using very sharp scissors, cut around the outline of each shape. Set all pieces aside, handling as little as possible to minimize fraying.

Cut one piece of fabric 10½" deep and 12" wide for the top of the background. Cut another piece 4¾" deep and 12" wide for the bottom. Following the instructions on the spray adhesive (and protecting the surrounding area with newspapers) spray the wrong side of these two pieces. Smooth the top piece onto the matboard, leaving no wrinkles; then apply the bottom piece so that the edges of the two pieces overlap. Spray the wrong sides of the other cut-outs, placing them as shown. Draw a mouth on the bear's face with a marking pen.

To make ribbon on the packages, draw thin lines of glue on the fabric with the point of a toothpick. Criss-cross short lengths of embroidery floss over the glue to make ribbons and glue on a bow also made of floss. Cut a mat to fit and insert the finished collage in a purchased frame.★

AN EASY DECORATION

Nothing could be simpler, or more effective, than this door decoration made of pine cones and bright red ribbon. Make a large bow from about 5 yards of weather-resistant velvet ribbon (3"-wide), catching the loops at the center with a length of floral wire. Attach long streamers with another length of wire. Bend the ends of both wires into a loop for hanging. Clip the ends of the streamers into an attractive notched shape.

Wrap a piece of floral wire around the base of 4 large pine cones, twisting these wires around each streamer several inches from the bottom. Clip the ends of the wires.★

DON'T BURN THESE LOGS

These deer and the shepherd with sheep started their lives in the woodpile! With bodies made from logs and legs made from smaller branches, they seem almost alive as they nibble the grass or stand poised with ears alert. You may vary the positions (and personalities!) of the animals a great deal by changing the angle at which you insert the legs, neck, and antlers.

Both the deer and sheep are constructed alike. Begin with a log for the body; about two feet long is a good size. Cut a short length of a slightly smaller log to act as a head. Leave the head with straight-cut ends, or round the nose if you have the facilities for turning wood. (You may also whittle the nose into a rounded shape.)

Drill each log for the body in four places for the legs, using a drill with a 1" bit. (See the diagram for placement. The holes should be at least 1½" deep.) Drill other holes at the top front of the body for a neck and under the head where the neck joins.

The legs and neck are made from lengths of sturdy branches (approximately 1½" in diameter). Legs for the deer should be long and spindly, while those for the sheep should be shorter. Cut the branches for the legs to size and taper one end of each slightly with a knife. Cut another branch for the neck and taper it at both ends. Insert all branches in their respective holes, add the head, and adjust the way the animal stands by sawing off the legs if necessary.

For the deer, choose two branches of a similar size to use as antlers—they should have several forks at the top for the best effect. Drill holes at the top of the head to hold them in position; then insert the antlers. Add a tiny branch for a tail if desired. To dress a boy deer, tie a large bow around the neck. For a girl deer, tie a bow around the neck, but add smaller bows to antlers as well.

Make the woolly covering for the sheep from artificial fur (available at fabric stores). Begin with a rectangular piece large enough to stretch from the tail end of the log to the forehead. Slit the fur on each side, where the neck changes its angle, so that the fur will bend. Trim the edges for ears as shown in the photograph.

Make the body of the shepherd from a log about six feet long. Photographed in New Mexico, the one in the photograph is cedar, but any hardwood or pine log would do as well. Drill a hole in each side and insert two smaller branches to use as arms. Drape a blanket over the shoulders or insert the arms through the sleeves of an old coat. Add a hat of whatever type you choose. (Here, an old black hat was trimmed with yarn braids before it was put on the shepherd.) Cut a tall sapling and lean it against the arm to act as a shepherd's staff.★

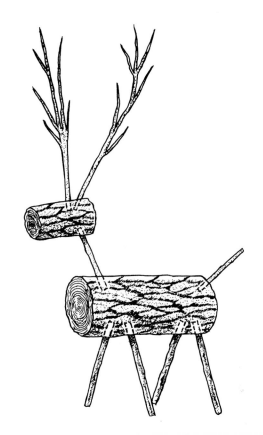

AN ARMLOAD OF GREENERY

When it is time to "deck the halls," garlands are among the best decorations you could choose. There is something about a home swagged with lush ropes of greenery that lifts it above the ordinary. Garlands may be draped across a mantel, over the doors, up a staircase, above a painting, or even around the columns; wherever they are used they add a richness and traditional feeling hard to duplicate by other means.

The photographs here show two entirely different decorating styles, both done with garlands. In one home, swags of evergreen clippings are draped down both sides of a staircase. With understated elegance, the newel posts are trimmed with large bows of shrimp-colored taffeta ribbon and fans made from the palmetto leaves found in coastal areas. The heat in most houses will make greenery dry out within a week—to prolong the life of your indoor garland, turn down the temperature whenever possible.

Simple garlands of unadorned long-leaf pine are wrapped around the porch columns of a log house, with more draped over the entrance. Large, matching wreaths hung on both sides of the door are trimmed with bright red bows. These decorations will last for several weeks outside in the cool weather.

Many types of greenery may be used in making garlands—from pine and juniper, to cedar and spruce, to the more formal boxwood or magnolia. (Some nurseries sell lengths of ready-made garland during the Christmas season for those who don't have the time to make it themselves.) Clippings from the bottom of too-tall Christmas trees might be used if you have enough of them, but garlands in general take more greenery than one would think!

Even newly-cut evergreens should be conditioned before they are used in order to make them stay fresh as long as possible. To do this, place the cut branches in a bucket of water after crushing the base of their stems with a hammer or slitting the base

Add a holiday flourish to your bird feeder by topping it with a bright bow. Don't be surprised if suspicious little birds wait a few hours before coming to sample the refreshments.

with a sharp knife. Leave the branches in the water overnight in a cool place, so that they will absorb as much as possible.

If the garland will be used where there is a possibility that the sap flowing from the cut stems might damage the wall, you might take the extra precaution of dipping the end of each stem in melted candle wax after conditioning.

Garlands are made by two main methods, no matter which type of plant material is

31

used. The more traditional method begins with a long piece of rope, preferably colored green. Short lengths of branches are wired to this rope with a continuous spool of florist's wire. The rope adds weight to the garland and enables you to make a well-defined scalloped pattern; it is used mainly with boxwood or pittosporum clippings.

The other method is similar, but no rope is used. Instead, each branch is wrapped with a continuous wire, then joined to another, with the leafy end of the first one overlapping the stem end of the next to hide it. Both methods work well, but unless you have made an exceptionally full garland, you may still need to tuck in a few clippings to hide the wire once the garland is hung.

If you need support for the garland, or must keep it in place for a long time, consider installing several metal cup hooks where the holes would not be noticed. Tiny nails placed along the top edge of a door frame may also be used and may be removed later with no visible damage to the frame.★

THIS WREATH IS DIFFERENT

Most vine wreaths are a natural brown color, which is fine if you are adding trimmings, but not so fine if you'd like to have a spot of color on your wall or door. Here is a wreath with a new twist—although it appears to be made of vines, it still has green leaves, even months after it is made.

Not every vine or flexible twig will dry so successfully; most will lose their leaves or turn to a dull brown color. This longer lasting wreath is made from the graceful, arching branches of the shrub elaeagnus, which is also known as silverberry. When freshly made, as shown on the wall, the wreath is green with a faintly silver underside on the leaves. As they dry, the green leaves become a little darker but, unless handled roughly, they remain attached. The wreath on the door is the same one on the wall, but it was photographed several months later.

To make a wreath, cut four or five long branches of elaeagnus. Form one of them into a circular shape of the desired size, wrapping the last few inches around the rest of the wreath to hold it together. Continue adding one branch at a time, wrapping around and through the others as you go. Hang the wreath as is, or add a bow, a few berries, or other trimmings.★

HONEYSUCKLE – THE VERSATILE VINE

Once you have made a wreath or two, you may think that you have exhausted the possibilities of decorating with vines for the holidays. Think again! These stunning decorations are made of nothing more than ordinary honeysuckle vines—the kind that grow rampant on fences and trees across America.

The figures are constructed much like wire sculptures—the basic form, similar to an armature, is made by bending several vines into shape. More vines are wrapped around this form to hold it in place and give thickness where needed. Short ends of the vines are laced in and out of the longer vines, so that the finished piece is woven together like a basket and will not fall apart with use. The best vine sculptures come from practice, of course, but even beginners can have excellent results.

Figures may be either free-standing or attached to a vine wreath, as shown by the reindeer in the photograph. (For some added color, poke small bits of greenery around the edge of the wreath.) By weaving the vines so that there is a depression in the center, the sculpture may be used as a container for flowers or fruits, as shown above.

Some general tips will make it easier to start. Gather the vines while they are still growing and flexible. You will need both medium and fine vines, with leaves stripped off, for most projects. There is no need to soak the vines in water before using them as long as they are supple.

Leave the bark on, unless you desire a bleached appearance, such as that in the figure of Baby Jesus. For the lighter vines, coil some in a large pot of water and simmer for

two or three hours. Remove them and, while
the vine is still warm, hold one end in your
hand while pulling a rough rag down the
length of the vine. The bark will peel off,
leaving the white, woody portion beneath.

The most common mistake is for someone
making sculptures to be afraid of breaking
the vines. Do not hesitate to bend, pull,
push and otherwise force the unruly vines
into shape. The worst that can happen is that
the vine occasionally will indeed break, but
you can weave in the broken ends and cover
the break with another vine.

When you are satisfied with the sculpture,
you may start using it right away. It will dry
naturally and retain its shape if you have
laced it together as directed. To clean the
sculpture, either let the shower run on it or
douse it with water from a hose.

WAITING FOR THE MAIL

A mailbox is seen by your neighbors as often as they pass by your house. This year, greet them with a cheerfully decorated mailbox—your postman will enjoy it too!

Although the shape of your particular mailbox may call for different placement of the decorations, general instructions are the same. Begin with a block of plastic foam, tinted green. Attach it firmly to the mailbox by wrapping it with fine florist's wire (place something soft, such as a folded cloth, beneath the foam to minimize scratching). Insert short lengths of greenery to form a pleasing arrangement, adding clumps of berries if you like.

Choose weatherproof ribbon to make your bows—other kinds simply do not hold up well in the rain and wind. Make one large bow, or a smaller one for each side, wiring these in place.★

A WISH FOR THE WORLD

Announce your heartfelt sentiments with this banner made to hang outside. Hung from a tree or beside your door, it is a lovely way to wish your neighbors a Merry Christmas.

The dove and olive leaves, symbols of peace, are machine-appliquéd to the deep blue background. If you are careful in choosing your fabrics, the banner may stay out in all kinds of weather.

YOU WILL NEED:
pattern on page 139
fabric (45"-wide) in the following colors:
  1⅝ yds. deep blue
  ½ yd. gold
  ⅛ yd. red
  ⅓ yd. green
  ⅝ yd. white
thread to match all fabrics

41" (½"-diameter) wooden dowel
42" (⅝"-wide) wooden dowel
2 metal screw-eyes (½"-wide)
1¼ yds. strong cotton cord

The best fabric for outdoor use is nylon bunting, which may be purchased from a sailmaker's shop or a flag-maker. If this is unavailable in your area, use any lightweight nylon or polyester, or a durable cotton/polyester blend such as sailcloth or duck. For indoor use, you might choose more formal fabrics such as moiré or taffeta.

Cut blue fabric into a rectangle (see pattern; using a cutting board marked in inches will help). Enlarge patterns for details and transfer to appropriate fabric. Cut all letters from gold fabric, berries from red, leaves from green, and body and wing of dove from white.

Place letters on blue background and pin in position, keeping letters at least 3" from lower edge and 4" away from side edges (see photograph). Baste by hand just inside the edges. Center dove and arrange leaves and berries, pinning and basting as directed.

Using thread to match appliqué, sew around each piece with a wide zigzag stitch to cover edges. Trim any raveled threads that show.

Finish both sides by folding the edges ½", then ½" again (toward back), pinning as you go. Stitch close to inside fold. Finish bottom edge by folding ¼" toward back; stitch. Fold 1½" and stitch along first line of stitching to make a casing. Finish top in same manner, folding ¼" and then 2½" to make a larger casing.

Insert smaller dowel at bottom; baste ends of casing together to enclose. Insert a screw eye at each end of larger dowel; place dowel in top casing with eyes protruding from edges. Knot cord through eye on each side to serve as a hanger.★

CHANDELIER CHIC

Usually hanging in a prominent position, directly above a dining room table or in an entrance hall, a beautifully lit chandelier is an ideal spot for festive decorations. The rich gleam of metal and the sparkle of the bulbs makes a spotlight for an arrangement of green clippings and ribbon. Nothing could be any easier, because in most cases the branches are simply laid across the arms of the fixture and do not need to be attached.

Choose greenery with stiff stems—evergreens such as pine, fir, or holly, or even ivy vines work well. Cut clippings about ten or twelve inches long as a rule, but size them according to your own chandelier so that they cross two of the arms. Work your way around the fixture, adding one layer at a time until the desired fullness is reached, keeping the weight balanced so that the fixture hangs correctly.

Twine bright ribbon around and through the greenery as an accent. Some other variations: spray the greenery with artificial snow before it is arranged; add berries, small ornaments, or tiny wooden toys; add a large bow with streamers at the center; or add small bows under each light.

An even more unusual treatment, shown in the photograph, is the addition of bright red apples hanging from ribbons tied to each arm. To do this, insert a wooden florist's pick in the top of each apple, going through one end of a short length of ribbon. Add a bow at the top of the apple to cover the pick and tie the ribbon to the arm of the fixture. Caution children not to eat apples stuck with picks—dyes in some picks are poisonous.★

WELCOMING WINDOWS

When well-decorated, a window can be one of the most inviting spots in your home. Those people looking out will see the landscape framed by a pleasant vignette, while those looking in will see the warmly lit room behind a window on which you have obviously spent some thought. The windows on these pages represent only two ideas—use them as inspiration for creating your own decorations.

The larger window, above, acts as a backdrop for a colorful display of winter fruits. There are apples, oranges, pears, nuts and berries—nature's bounty heaped in bowls and baskets. Such a large display is probably too impractical, despite its simple theme, for everyday use. It would be ideal for a large party, though, and guests could help themselves to the edible decorations. If you would prefer to display something other than perishable fruits, the same boxes and baskets could be used with bright ornaments, balls of yarn, stacks of presents, or bunches of cut greenery mixed with poinsettias or other flowering plants.

To add a homey touch, place a few small branches of greenery (cut from the base of your tree) at the base of the window. Add an electrified candle at the center and an accent of crisp, red apples and ribbon.

The smaller window, below, has a decoration which is easily made, yet may be saved from year to year. A large cone from a white pine tree acts as a base for tiny alder cones, plaid ribbon, German statice, and a bright red cardinal glued on top. The cone was heated, before it was decorated, in a very low temperature oven until the pitch inside was released and gave it a glazed appearance. (You may eliminate this step and spray the cone with lacquer instead.)

Add a loop of golden cord and hang the ornament from the lock on the window. Hide the lock with some cut evergreen branches. When the season is over, wrap the cone carefully and save it until next year.★

A SPRINKLING OF SNOWFLAKES

When nights turn cool, and the best way to spend an evening is in front of the fire, then it is time to begin a good needlework project. This small quilt, with its design of winter snowflakes, is easy for beginners because it is pieced by machine and does not need to be quilted on a frame. When finished, the quilt measures approximately 34 inches by 48 inches, an ideal size for a wallhanging or just right to cover a napping child.

YOU WILL NEED:
patterns on page 139
100% cotton fabric:
  ½ yd. each rust and blue mini-dot print
  ½ yd. stripe
  ¼ yd. rust
  ⅝ yd. white or off-white
  1½ yds. deep blue (extra fabric required for length)
  1½ yds. white fabric for backing
crib-sized quilt batting
white quilting thread
46" dowel (1"-diameter)
2 metal hooks and eyes

Prewash and iron all fabrics before cutting. These measurements include a ¼" seam allowance on all sides.
CUT: 12 (1½" x 12½") strips in each print
      7 (2½" x 12½") strips in stripe
      2 (2½") center squares in rust
      6 (10½") squares in white
      6 (9") squares in print for snowflakes (3 in each color)
      2 (4" x 40½") blue border strips
      2 (4" x 26½") blue border strips
      4 (4") corner squares in rust
      4 (1½" x 50") binding strips (trim later)

ASSEMBLING: Fold 9" squares into quarters and place snowflake patterns on folded edges. Trace and cut 6 snowflakes; baste one snowflake onto each 10½" square. Turn under seam allowance and appliqué in place. Machine-stitch 1½" x 12½" strips around each block, using the same print as the snowflake and mitering the corners.

Stitch one 2½" x 12½" strip of striped fabric between two different colored blocks (you will have three rows of blocks). Sew a 2½" square between the ends of two 2½" x 12½" strips to make one that is long and narrow. Repeat with remaining matching strips. Sew these narrow strips between rows of blocks, positioning blocks with alternating colors. Sew a 4" x 40½" border strip to each long side of appliquéd piece. Sew one 4" square to each end of 4" x 26½" border strips; then sew to short sides of appliqué.

Cut backing and batting 4" larger than completed work. Spread backing on flat surface, with batting on top. Center appliquéd piece on both layers, facing up, and pin in place. Baste temporarily through all three layers with bright thread, spacing rows of stitching 5" apart vertically and horizontally. (This holds layers in place while you quilt; stitches will be removed.)

QUILTING: For each square, quilt around snowflake about ⅛" inside edge; repeat with a row in "ditch" next to snowflake. Outline quilt around snowflake, leaving about ⅜" between rows. Continue quilting until rows fill white squares (see photograph above).

Quilt around edges of white blocks and around outer edges of 1"-wide strips. Quilt along center of all 2" strips, forming a cross in center of 2" squares as you go.

Border: Quilt in 3" x 4" diamonds with a smaller 2" x 3" diamond inside. (There will be six diamonds on each short end, with a space left open in the middle. There will be eight diamonds on each long side, with a ninth diamond positioned in the middle.) Corners have a double-row square, measuring 2¼" outside and 1½" inside, placed on the diagonal.

BINDING: Trim batting and backing so that they extend evenly ¼" over front side. Pin binding strips to front, right sides together, trimming ends to fit each side. Stitch binding in place with a ¼" seam. Turn to back. Turn under ¼" hem and pin. Slipstitch in place, hemming ends of binding as well. Remove temporary basting stitches.

Sew 4"-long loops, made from scraps, every 6" along top edge of wallhanging so that tops of loops are hidden. Insert a 46"-long dowel or broomstick through loops. Attach a metal eye at each end of dowel and hang from hooks on wall.★

GOLDEN HARVEST WREATH

Just as nature needs time to make a pine tree, some decorations take a little time to make, but will last for many years—this wreath is one of them. Made from cones gathered in the fall, the wreath is equally attractive in both a casual and sophisticated setting. The golden stalks of wheat are a striking contrast to the rich brown tones of the pinecones beneath.

To make this wreath, it is almost imperative that you have a hot glue gun, which is one of the handiest of all tools. The glue will harden almost instantly, allowing you to proceed with attaching the next cone without having to hold the previous one in position.

YOU WILL NEED:
14"-diameter wire wreath form
small pinecones (about 60)
1"-thick green plastic foam
6 or 7 cones from deodar cedar
hot glue gun
wheat (purchase at craft stores)
5 yds. heavy gold metallic cord
wire for hanging
clear acrylic spray

Wedge small pinecones firmly onto wire form to make tight circles around inner and outer rims. Cut small pieces of plastic foam, and wedge between the rings of cones to fill spaces roughly. Form rosettes from deodar cones; then arrange around wreath and glue. Cover any plastic foam that shows by gluing on individual deodar cone petals.

Clip extra stalks from wheat, leaving about ½" of stalk on the heads. Attach heads just beneath edge of cone rosettes with a dab of glue (see photograph for placement). Make a large golden bow with four long streamers, attaching loops with glue as you go. Hide center of bow with another cone rosette. Add a wire loop on back for hanging. Finish by spraying with clear acrylic.★

Pale wheat stands out dramatically from the darker-colored cones used as the background for this wreath. Golden cord is looped into a bow for an opulent accent.

FOR ST. LUCIA'S DAY

In Sweden, the celebration of St. Lucia's Day is almost as important as Christmas itself. Today, among Americans of Swedish descent, this day is often observed as part of the holiday season.

Lucia was a young girl born in Sicily who, according to legend, gave away her dowry money to help those in need. She is honored on her feast day, December 13, when girls dress in simple white "wedding" gowns and wear crowns of candles on their heads. As part of the celebration, the traditional sweet buns called "cats" are served. (A recipe for these appears on page 106.)

This vine wreath, with its doll-like figure of St. Lucia, is an appropriate gift for a girl of any age. The animals and flowers as well as St. Lucia are made of painted baker's clay. Her face is made in a mold of Sculpy®, formed on the face of an actual doll.

YOU WILL NEED:
Sculpy® modeling compound
hard plastic or ceramic doll with distinct features
recipe for baker's clay on page 88
corn starch
4" (16-gauge) wire
water color paints
1 skein embroidery floss (for hair)
white crepe paper and bits of lace
hot glue gun
assorted toy implements (broom, cooking utensils, wreath for head)
German statice or other dried flowers
toothpicks
vine wreath

The mold for the face is made from Sculpy® modeling compound, sold in craft stores. Firmly press a flattened circle of Sculpy® onto a plastic doll's face; then pull away gently, leaving a negative impression of facial features. (Make several of these molds.) Bake at 350° for 5 to 10 minutes.

Prepare recipe for baker's clay. Using this clay, roll a 1" x 4" cylinder for body. Cut lower part of cylinder to make legs. Dust mold with cornstarch; press clay inside to fill impressions, adding more at back of head. Remove mold, wet base, insert shortened toothpick for support, and join to body.

To make arms, roll two pencil-thin coils 1"-long. Flatten one end of each for hands and cut "fingers" with tiny scissors. Bend wire into a C-shape; insert an end into each arm, with thumbs pointing inward.

Mold extra clay into several small flowers, birds, and animals before baking. Bake all clay pieces on foil or a cookie sheet in a 225° oven for 3 hours, (until hard but still light in color). Allow to cool.

Paint face and hands with skin-tone watercolors. Draw sleeping eyes on face and add a mouth and rosy cheeks. (Avoid harsh facial features.) Make hair by wrapping embroidery floss around head and gluing in place. Cut 1½"-wide strips of crepe paper, using these to wrap body, wire, and upper arms to give them extra fullness.

To make dress, cut a strip of crepe paper (12" x 20") with grain running parallel to 12" side. Fold in half so that it measures 6" x 20"; gather folded edge with white thread to fit around neck. Cut another piece of crepe paper (5½" x 20") with grain parallel to 5½" side. Fold 1" toward back and gather folded edge around neck for overskirt.

Cut a piece of crepe paper 4" x 6". Beginning on 6" side, wrap around wire and arms to cover, leaving hands showing. Tightly wrap white thread at cuffs to hold. Tack sleeves to back of dress with thread. Add a collar made from a scrap of gathered lace.

Finish figure with a tiny crown, purchased or made from wire and trimmed with small flowers. Glue on candles made by dipping ends of toothpicks in red paint. Add little baskets, brooms, or other trimmings.

WREATH: Paint clay flowers, birds, and animals in colors to complement St. Lucia figure. Glue to vine wreath and fill in bare spots with bits of dried flowers. Add tiny kitchen implements if desired. Wire or glue St. Lucia figure to center of wreath.★

LAST-MINUTE IDEAS

You may have some decorations right at your fingertips—items that you have never even thought of using! Some craftswomen, who are so used to thinking of the craft potential of various materials, are apt to overlook the decorative potential of the same materials. Try to see your supplies with a new eye this Christmas; some of them should be taken out of their boxes and put to use decorating your home.

Consider the possibilities of sewing supplies—the multi-colored beauty of threads, the intricate weaves of ribbons and braids, and the diversity of a button collection might all become important elements in a holiday arrangement.

Choose your most colorful buttons to fill an assortment of glass containers. Tie several lengths of ribbon around the top of each jar; then tie into bows. Anyone who sews seems to accumulate an assortment of spools of thread—these look lovely placed in baskets against a background of candles, shown here in candleholders made of wooden bobbins.

Other craft supplies have equally pleasing colors and shapes—balls of yarn and folded fabrics, jars of paint and interesting papers—use your imagination to create a still-life arrangement featuring them. Your decorations will be unique and so appropriate to your craft-loving lifestyle.

Other decorations may be made from some of the items that you have collected over the years. In the photograph opposite, an assortment of unmatched goblets is put to use holding votive candles. Arranged on a brass tray with a mirror behind, the facets of the crystal reflect the flickering of the candles in a spectacular display of light.

A collection of shells and sea urchins is lovely in a tabletop decoration. Here, a hand-beaten copper bowl with a handle made of antlers is filled with the pastel shells. Woven through the arrangement is a string of tiny white lights, which twinkle as they illuminate the shells and the delicate baby's breath tucked around the edges.★

DECOY DECORATIONS

Whether he is a sportsman, a collector, or just a nature-lover, the man in your life is bound to appreciate a handsome holiday arrangement of decoys. If he, like many men, admits to a preference for "outdoor-type" decorations rather than those that are based on elves, Santas, reindeer, or other whimsical themes—then here is a chance to give him his wish.

If you are lucky enough to possess some decoys, antique or not, you can use them as the basis for an entire arrangement. The top of any tall chest, a library table, a piano, or even a bookcase shelf is a good setting. Combine the decoys with boxes or books or a tall vase of greenery to form a pleasing composition. Fill in with more greenery or berries tucked around the base.

For a larger arrangement, such as that shown on the mantel, you may want to add a little "filler" to make the decoys you have look more substantial. Here, excelsior packing material was made into "nests" along the length of the mantel before the decoys were placed. Candles in candlesticks are always appropriate, but some of your other accessories might hold a candle safely as well. Consider placing candles in small cups, muffin tins, glasses, or as in this case, a candle-mold. (Anchor the base of the candle in florist's clay if there is no indentation to hold it securely.)★

SIMPLE TOUCHES

Sometimes it is not so much what you do, but *how* you do it, that counts. You can spend a great deal of money on ready-made decorations from a fancy store, or you can use a little imagination and turn your own accessories into equally appealing decorations—for free.

A dark corner that needs a little brightening can usually benefit from candles—the more, the better. You can create an interesting display by stacking boxes (in this case, antique Shaker boxes) of graduating sizes, tied together with ribbon and topped with a large bow. A stack of gaily wrapped presents might be tied together in the same way for even more color. Green branches cost little or nothing, but do more than anything else to add a lift to your decorations.

If you have a few baskets, put them to use! In one home, a split oak basket, woven by craftsmen in the hills of Tennessee, is filled with greenery and sprays of bright red nandina berries. Another is filled with some roasted peanuts to eat by the fire. The third, a coiled grass "gullah" basket made near Charleston, South Carolina, is filled with assorted pinecones. A simple idea, costing nothing, but it is certainly as appealing a decoration as one could wish.★

A HOST OF ANGELS

Making this dazzling decoration is as easy as cutting paper dolls—or paper angels, to be more accurate! The fans behind the angels are just as easy; so even if your craft expertise is limited to folding, pasting, and cutting, you will be able to make this for your mantel or buffet.

Choose a paper that folds well, such as crisp typing paper, to make the angels. (Any fairly stiff paper will do, but cardboard or poster board is too thick.) Fold the paper accordion-fashion, with the pleats 1¼" wide. Using the pattern on page 133, transfer the outline of the angel to the first pleat; then cut all layers with sharp scissors along the solid lines. Glue several sets of angels together with white household glue to obtain the length needed. Leave the angels plain or add a line of glue and glitter around the edges.

To make the metallic fans, fold a strip of gift wrap lengthwise with wrong sides together. (You will need a piece of paper twice as long as the original width before folding.) Pleat the folded gift wrap (again, 1¼"-wide pleats) and tape or staple the raw-edged base together to form a fan. Make several fans in different sizes and combine to form various arrangements.

The decoration shown is made with three fans. The largest fan acts as a backdrop for the angel paper dolls, which are attached with double-faced tape at several points. The smaller fans add dimension to the arrangement, with one standing upright and one resting horizontally beneath some plastic balls covered with glitter.★

HANDMADE WITH LOVE

BEAUTIFUL BOXES

Do you need to make a gift for someone very dear to you? Fabric-covered wooden boxes are ideal for holding jewelry or other little treasures—just buy the box and add your special touches. The embroidered bunny or goose on the top is a delightfully whimsical accent for bedroom or bath.

The pincushion (page 54) is a variation of the boxes, minus the embroidery but with the dainty addition of ribbon roses. Make the set in matching fabrics for a gift that will be long-remembered.

YOU WILL NEED (to make each box):
chart on page 133
transfer pencil
remnants of two coordinating fabrics (striped and mini-print)
embroidery floss
oval "Shaker-style" wooden box (4½"-long)
4" x 6" polyester fleece
white household glue
⅛ yd. Stitch Witchery® fusible fabric bond
¾ yd. plus 1" (⅛"-wide) satin ribbon
14" (¼"- or ⅜"-wide) scalloped lace edging

Transfer the design to an 8"-square of mini-print fabric. Work design according to chart, using four strands of floss. (Work French knots on goose box with eight strands of floss. Outline both bunny and two geese with small straight stitches using only one strand of floss.) Block finished stitchery.

Turn embroidered side down; center top of box over design and trace around lid. Add ½" to traced outline and cut an oval. Clip around edge every ½", cutting almost to traced line. Trace around top of box again on polyester fleece; cut oval exactly on this line.

Place fleece on wrong side of embroidery, aligning ovals. Apply thin layer of glue to side of box lid. Position lid upside down on fleece and press clipped edges onto glued surface, smoothing them as you work.

Cut a strip of striped fabric twice as wide as side of box lid and as long as distance around box lid plus ½ inch. Cut a strip of fusible fabric bond to same length, but only half as wide. Fold fabric strip lengthwise with right sides out; press. Insert fusible fabric bond in crease and press again.

Place lid on box. Cut a second strip of both fabric and fusible bond to go around side of box showing below lid (follow instructions as given in the paragraph above, changing measurements). Glue narrow strip to side of lid and wider strip to side of box, with raw edges toward bottom. Trim away overhanging fabric.

Glue a strip of narrow ribbon around bottom of both box and lid to cover edge of fabric; add lace trimming around lid.

YOU WILL NEED (for pincushion):
wooden box (2¼"-diameter)
scraps of polyester batting
scraps of mini-print fabric
scrap of Stitch Witchery® fusible fabric bond
white household glue
⅔ yd. (⅛"-wide) satin ribbon
½ yd. (⅜"-wide) lace edging
⅔ yd. (⅝"-wide) satin ribbon (for flowers)
3" (⅛"-wide) green ribbon (for leaves)

Tiny wooden boxes with lids may be purchased at most craft stores which stock tole painting supplies. Lid is not used in making pincushion; remove and discard or reserve for another project.

Cut five or six 3"-diameter circles from batting. Press circles into box firmly, smoothing top layer to form a gentle mound.

Trace bottom of box on wrong side of printed fabric. Add ½" allowance and cut circle. Clip every ½" almost to traced line. Apply a layer of glue to top rim of box (part that would normally be covered by lid). Position fabric circle on batting and press clipped edge onto glue, cutting away excess fabric. Glue lace edging around box to cover raw edge; then glue ⅛"-wide ribbon along straight edge of lace as shown.

Cut a strip of fabric as long as distance around box plus ½"; it should be twice as wide as side of box up to groove. Fold this strip lengthwise, wrong sides facing, and press. Insert a strip of fusible bond, only half as wide, and press. Glue strip around box with raw edges on bottom. Glue lace around top of this fabric strip. Trim at top and bottom with narrow ribbon (see photograph).

Make four ribbon roses from satin ribbon according to instructions given below. Glue an "X" of pale green ribbon to top of pincushion; then glue on roses.

RIBBON ROSES: Thread needle with thread to match ribbon. Fold six to eight inches of ⅝"-wide satin ribbon lengthwise. Fold one end of ribbon at a 90° angle with 1½" of ribbon remaining on shorter end (see diagram). Hold shorter end with right hand and longer end with left hand. Wrap longer end tightly around fold to form center of bud, taking stitches in several places at base to hold ribbon. Continue wrapping, but twist ribbon, getting looser as you wrap so that the flower appears to open. When enough petals have been added, wrap thread very tightly around base and take stitch through base to secure. Clip threads and trim remaining ribbon.★

WREATHED IN OLD LACE

Feminine, fanciful, and ever so romantic, this heirloom-quality wreath is a lovely way to use those bits and pieces of lace that you have been saving. Use the wreath as a pillow on your guestroom bed at Christmas, or hang it on the wall throughout the year.

This wreath is much easier to make than it appears—its intricate appearance comes from the variety of textures in the lace, the ruffles, and the featherstitching used as ornamentation. The lace does not have to match; in fact, some lovely effects may be obtained by combining both white and ecru laces. If you have no scraps, piece together lengths of flat lace edging to form a fabric large enough for each section.

YOU WILL NEED:
pattern on page 144
stitch guide on page 123
wide paper for making wreath pattern
½ yd. (36"- to 45"-wide) satin fabric
16 lace scraps—each approximately 5" x 7"
4 yds. (3½"-wide) lace (or 1⅔ yds. if pregathered)
1⅓ yds. (1"-wide) lace (or ⅔ yd. if pregathered)
2¼ yds. (¾"-wide) lace for trimming
2½ yds. (1"-wide) double-faced ribbon
rayon floss (Marlitt®)
1 bag (16 oz.) polyester stuffing
1 plastic curtain ring (for hanging)

Make wreath pattern by cutting a 16" circle from paper. Fold circle in half, then in half again—continuing until you have 16 equal sections. Draw another circle 3" from center; cut along line to make a 6"-wide hole in middle.

Using whole wreath as a pattern and *allowing an extra ⅜" seam allowance on both inner and outer edges,* cut 2 pieces from satin fabric. Cut 16 wedge-shaped pieces of lace according to pattern (page 144); join them with machine stitching as shown to form a third circle. Place wrong side of assembled lace on right side of satin circle,

pin, and baste together along inner and outer edges with a ¼" seam (ease to fit; then treat as one piece). Press. Embroider featherstitching along each seam where lace sections are joined.

Gather lace to size if necessary. Pin 3½"-wide lace to outer edge of top; pin 1"-wide lace to inner edge, with gathered sides of lace ⅜" from raw edges. (All ungathered edges of lace will face toward fabric.) Baste lace, clip seam allowance along inner circle, and press so that inner lace faces center.

Baste along inner edge of remaining satin circle with a ⅜" seam, clip, and press seam allowance toward wrong side. Pin top to back, right sides together; sew around outer edge. Clip seam, turn right side out, and press with outer ruffle on the edge.

Pin top and bottom together along inner edge with ruffle toward center. Blindstitch two pieces together behind ruffle, about ¾ of way around, leaving an opening for stuffing. Stuff wreath; then blindstitch opening closed. Add lace trim or tatting to cover seams where inner and outer ruffles are attached, tacking trim by hand.

To make bow, wrap ribbon around a 6"-wide piece of cardboard 5 times, leaving two 6"-long ends free. Tie tightly around middle of loops with another length of ribbon, again leaving two long ends. Tack bow in place at bottom of wreath and clip ends diagonally to desired lengths. Sew curtain ring to back of wreath if you plan to hang.★

FRÈRE JACQUES

Friendly enough to entrance a child, yet appealing to adult tastes also, this beguiling clown doll is a sweet blend of innocent charm and sophistication. Because his costume, with its dusky colors and wide laces, is so reminiscent of a courtly jester, he has an endearing and old-fashioned appearance.

This doll is firmer than most cloth dolls, with stuffing packed tightly into some parts of the arms, legs, and body and loosely into other parts. Knowing just where to pack tightly is one of the secrets of his distinctive appearance. Because of the way they are sectioned, both arms and legs are very flexible and the doll has a "floppy" manner of moving. His clothes are tacked to his body and may be removed only by clipping stitches.

YOU WILL NEED:
patterns on pages 125-127
½ yd. white woven fabric (for body, bottom, and arms)
¼ yd. woven fabric (for hat and legs)
12" x 12" white knit fabric (for head)
½ yd. woven fabric (for suit)
thread to match all fabrics
polyester stuffing
heavy duty carpet thread
small amount of embroidery floss (blue, light brown, flesh)
yarn (for hair)
scrap of black felt (for shoes)
2 yds. (1¾"-wide) lace
1 skein embroidery floss (for tassels)
⅞ yd. (¼"-wide) velvet ribbon
1 yd. (⅝"-wide) satin ribbon

Transfer all patterns to the appropriate fabrics, noticing how many of each piece you will need. The lines you have drawn will be your sewing lines. *Allowing an extra ⅜" on all sides,* cut each piece from fabric and set aside until needed. Note that all machine sewing is to be done in thread to match the fabric, while all hand sewing is done with a doubled strand of carpet thread.

BODY: With right sides facing, sew sides of body together, keeping neck and bottom open. Turn right side out. Stuff very firmly, pushing in as much as you can. Turn under seam allowance on bottom, pin to bottom of body, and whipstitch around edge.

To make each leg, place two pieces with right sides facing and sew around all but top edge. Turn right sides out. Stuff lower part of leg firmly; sew across on broken line. Stuff upper leg lightly, turn top edge under, and sew shut. Whipstitch leg to front of body as shown on pattern. Repeat for other leg.

To make each arm, place two pieces with right sides facing and sew around edges, leaving seam open. Turn, stuff hand very lightly, and sew along broken lines to form fingers. Continue stuffing (firmly) to next broken line, sew across line, stuff remainder of arm lightly, close, and sew across line. Attach to body by whipstitching (see diagram).

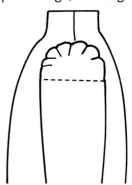

FACE: With right sides of knit fabric pieces together, stitch around head, leaving only neck open. Stuff firmly; then close neck by making a row of running stitches around the opening (with carpet thread) and pulling tight to close. Sew head to body by hand, hiding all rough edges.

Draw facial features on stuffed head and embroider in colors shown, using satin stitch for eyes and nose, backstitch for mouth, and straight stitch for eyebrows.

To make hair, wrap yarn 60 times around a 12"-long piece of paper. Machine stitch across middle, remove paper, position yarn on head, arrange yarn evenly, and glue in place. Trim yarn into a "page-boy" style—cut straight all around with bangs in front.

CLOTHES: To make each shoe, sew top pattern piece at back, matching notches. Attach top of shoe to sole by sewing around edges of both with a ⅛" outside seam. Place shoe on foot and tack to hold at back. Wrap embroidery floss 10 times around a 2"-long piece of cardboard, tie middle, clip ends, and tack to toe to form a tassel.

Place two hat pieces with right sides facing and sew around top and sides. Fold hat across middle, matching dots, and sew dart across top of both pieces as shown. Turn up 1¼" to form a hem at bottom. Make two parallel rows of wide satin stitching around bottom of hat, letting one row cover raw edge of hem. Turn right side out. Make two tassels as instructed above for shoe tassels, and attach at top corners. Turn up the brim of hat.

To make clown suit, sew two front pieces together and then two back pieces together, with right sides facing. Join front to back by sewing inner seams of each leg together. Turn under ¼" to form a hem on each leg; then sew a length of lace to right side of each hem. Sew side seams of each leg together as far as "X".

Turn under ¼" to form hem on each sleeve, again applying a length of lace to cover hem. With right sides together, stitch each sleeve along underarm seam from hem to "X". Turn right side out and pin to body of suit with right sides together, matching "X"s. Sew each sleeve to body in one continuous seam. Hem top of suit. Apply lace to cover hem, this time with scalloped edge of lace pointing down toward suit.

ASSEMBLY: Slip suit onto clown's body. Using a double strand of carpet thread, make running stitches by hand around all openings just above lace; draw up tightly and fasten off, taking a stitch through clown at a seamline to hold suit in place. Cut velvet ribbon in half and make a bow around cuff of each leg. Tie another bow made from satin ribbon around neck just below lace collar.★

KEEP WARM IN STYLE

On cold blustery days, or on days when the winter sunlight peeks from behind a cloud, this knitted mohair cap and ascot will keep you warm. Although both garments are easy enough for beginning knitters, even experienced knitters find them perfect for gifts because they take so little time to complete.

The pin holding the brim is an attractive addition to the outfit. Wire loops of ⅛"-wide ribbon to tiny cones, a sprig of artificial cedar, and lacquered berries; then attach with hot glue to a purchased stickpin.

YOU WILL NEED (for cap):
three (50 gm balls) Neveda's Celesta (50% wool, 50% mohair, #2020 Blush) with 10" dp knitting needles (size 10 or size needed to obtain gauge)
or substitute five (25 gm skeins) Sunbeam Mohair (Dusk 216) with 10" dp knitting needles (size 9 or size needed to obtain gauge)
tapestry needle

GAUGE: In St st, on size 9 needles, 4 sts = 1", 5 rows = 1".

CAP: Cast on 80 sts loosely. Distribute evenly over 3 dp needles (26, 26, 28 sts). Be careful not to twist sts on first round. Work around in knit for 15".
To shape crown: *Rnd 1*: K 2 tog around (40 sts). *Rnd 2*: Knit. Work even in knit for 3 rows. *Rnds 6 through 9*: Rep Rnds 1 and 2 twice (10 sts). End yarn leaving a long tail. Thread yarn into needle and slip off the 10 sts as if to purl. Draw up and secure.
FINISHING: With purl side out, turn up cuff (knit side) 5". Loosely tack edge of cuff to hat. To wear, roll cuff up so that it covers tacked edge. Hold with decorative pin.

YOU WILL NEED (for ascot):
two (50 gm balls) Nevada's Celesta (50% wool, 50% mohair, #2020 Blush) with two dp needles (size 10 or size needed to obtain gauge)
or substitute three (25 gm skeins) Sunbeam Mohair (Dusk 216) with two dp needles (size 10 or size needed to obtain gauge)
tapestry needle

GAUGE: In garter st, on size 10 needles, 7 sts = 2", 12 rows = 2"
NOTE: In garter st, 2 rows = 1 ridge.

SCARF: Cast on 6 sts. *Row 1*: Knit. *Row 2*: K 1, inc 1 st in next st, k to last 2 sts, inc 1 st in next st, k 1. Rep Rows 1 and 2 until 28 sts. Work even for 22 rows. *Next Row*: K 2 tog across (14 sts). Work in k 1, p 1 ribbing for 12 rows. *Next Row*: Inc 1 st in each st across row (28 sts). Work even in garter st for 20".
To make Ascot Loop: To open loop, slip stitches alternately to two dp needles. Work stitches on one needle in k 1, p 1 ribbing for 12 rows. Rep for stitches on second needle. To close loop, knit across replacing all stitches on one needle, alternating stitches in same way they were slipped off. Work even in garter st for 22 rows.
To shape End: *Row 1*: K 1, SKP, k to last 3 sts, k 2 tog, k 1. *Row 2*: Knit. Rep Rows 1 and 2 until 6 sts. Bind off loosely; work in yarn ends neatly.
FINISHING: Fluff nap by brushing with a soft hairbrush.★

Standard Knitting Abbreviations	
k—knit	**rnd(s)**—round(s)
p—purl	**rep**—repeat
gm—gram	**inc**—increase
st(s)—stitch(es)	**dec**—decrease
tog—together	**dp**—double-pointed
St st—Stockinette stitch	
SKP—slip 1, knit 1, pass slipped stitch(es) over knit stitch(es)	
work even—means to work in stitch or pattern with no increases or decreases	

Figure 1

Figure 2

Figure 3

Figure 4

Hold ribbon as shown (figure 1), leaving enough ribbon hanging down on left side to form a small loop when bow is finished. Twist ribbon in center until it turns over and right side of ribbon is on top. Hold twist between left thumb and forefinger, with thumb on top.

Make a loop with long side of ribbon; twist ribbon again until it is right side up and catch it beneath your left thumb (figure 2). Make a loop on opposite side and twist again (figure 3).

Continue making loops, twisting each time, until bow is desired fullness. Wrap reserved end into a loop to cover your left thumb, holding cut end beneath that thumb. Twist a length of florist's wire around center to hold all loops tightly; top loop will hide wire and twists beneath it (figure 4). Gently pull loops to side for a more circular shape.

★★★

TIE THE PERFECT BOW

'Tis the season for bows on presents, bows on baskets, bows on wreaths, bows almost everywhere...but how do you make those beautiful, puffy bows? If your own bows are always looking droopy, try this never-fail method. The procedure works on any width of ribbon, but is best on those that are crisp, such as cut-edge floral ribbon. You may wish to practice on old scraps which have been ironed before you try it on fresh, new ribbon.

The technique is very simple—each time you complete a loop, you *twist* the ribbon one half turn around before you begin another loop so that the right side is always up. When your bow is as full as you like, wrap a wire around the center, twisting it to hold the loops in place. Follow the diagrams above, remembering always to hold the center of the bow with your left hand and to make new loops and twist with your right hand.

MRS. SANTA RECIPE HOLDER

Who is better qualified to hold a yummy Christmas recipe than Mrs. Santa herself? This painted figure is backed by a clothespin to hold your recipe card in view while you cook. For a unique gift, consider giving one of these holders, a stack of cards painted to match, your special recipe, and the goodies too! (Look on page 95 for the recipe for Glazed Spice Bars.)

After you have finished painting, glue a clothespin to the back as shown. If you would prefer to use Mrs. Santa as an ornament or a key holder, just leave off the clothespin and instead drill a small hole at the top of the hat.

YOU WILL NEED:
pattern on page 140
½"-thick wood (or substitute ¼"-thick birch veneer plywood)
jigsaw or band saw
sandpaper
wood sealer
Ceramcoat® acrylic paints

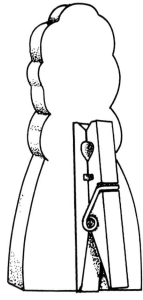

Color Chart
Georgia Clay
Ivory
Bright Red
Black
Maroon
Burnt Umber
Antique Gold
Christmas Green

brushes (liner, #6 or #8 flat, *old* #6 flat)
water-based varnish
spring-type clothespin
white household glue

Transfer outline to wood and cut shape with jigsaw or band saw. Sand edges; then apply sealer to front and back. Draw details on cut-out with pencil if necessary. A #6 or #8 flat brush is used throughout project—rinse brush well before each change of color.

Brush-mix Georgia Clay and Ivory to make a flesh color and paint teardrop-shaped face area. With Bright Red, apply a base coat to hat and dress, as well as entire back and sides of hat and dress. Allow paint to dry; apply second coat to these areas.

Side-load brush with very floated (or diluted) Bright Red. Make C-strokes under eyes for cheeks and paint suggestion of lower lip.

Brush-mix Black and Ivory to make shades of gray; paint both front and sides of hair. Side-load brush with floated Ivory and paint four or five downward strokes for apron, shading edges; then paint pocket and small plate.

Side-load brush with Maroon and Burnt Umber and shade around apron, hat, and arms. Dip corner of brush in Antique Gold; paint cupcake with L-stroke.

Switch to liner brush. With Burnt Umber, outline eyes, nose and mouth. Fill in eye area with Burnt Umber and highlight with Ivory and Black. Still using liner with Black, make glasses with four dots and broken lines (see photograph); then paint details on hat, arms, apron, plate, and cupcake.

Using worn-out #6 flat brush, stipple with Ivory and gray to make fur cuffs, collar, and hatband. Mix Ivory and Bright Red to make pink; stipple to make cupcake frosting. Apply 2 or 3 coats of varnish.★

A GIFT FOR THE BABY

Four happy-faced girls and boys will watch over your little one as he sleeps, and when he awakens, they'll be there ready to play with him. Tied across baby's bed within reach of his arms or legs, this soft, safe crib-kicker will stimulate your child and provide hours of amusement.

YOU WILL NEED:
patterns on page 145
¼ yd. (44"-wide) fabric for girls
¼ yd. (44"-wide) fabric for boys
scrap of fabric for pants
scrap of white fabric for faces
embroidery floss (red, blue, and white)
polyester stuffing
9 yds. each yellow and orange 4-ply yarn
2⅔ yds. (⅜"-wide) ribbon
¾ yd. (⅛"-wide) ribbon

Cut pattern pieces for front and back bodies and pants. Transfer patterns for faces to white fabric, but do not cut. Embroider features in backstitch with two strands of floss; cut faces. Using zigzag stitch, appliqué faces to body fronts (place face ¾" below top raw edge for girls, and ½" below edge for boys). Appliqué boys' pants to body fronts; then embroider two white "X"s on each pair of pants as shown.

Pin front and back pieces with right sides together. Sew with ⅜" seam, leaving all cuffs and bottom of each doll open for stuffing. Clip corners and curves, and turn bodies right side out. Stuff heads only.

To make girl's hair, fold five yards of yarn into 12" lengths, tie in middle, and tack to center of forehead. Tie again at each side 1¼" below center and tack at sides of face. Braid remaining yarn, tie at ends, and trim.

For boy's hair, fold 2 yards of yarn into 3" lengths. Tie in middle with yarn and tack to center of forehead. Trim hair as desired.

Fold ⅜"-wide ribbon in half, cut, and pin a large safety pin through both ribbons at one end. Use this pin to thread ribbons through both cuffs of all four dolls, leaving equal amounts of ribbon protruding from each end. Overlap cuffs, turning under ones on top to hide raw edges. Machine stitch across each cuff to hold ribbons in place.

Finish stuffing dolls and blindstitch bottom openings closed. Cut five 5" lengths of ⅛"-wide ribbon. Use these to tie small bows around each cuff; tack in place so that baby can't pull them off. Color cheeks with pink lipstick.

★★★

FOR COVERED DISH SUPPERS

If you are often invited to bring foods to a party yourself, then you know that balancing a hot casserole or keeping a salad from sliding off the seat of the car tends to diminish enthusiasm for such occasions. You'll never have a problem transporting any type of food if you take it in a quilted casserole carrier.

The shape of the holder adapts to fit most round, square, or oval casserole dishes as well as deep bowls—just pull the drawstring until you have a snug fit.

YOU WILL NEED:
pattern on page 144
½ yd. reversible prequilted fabric
1¾ yds. (⅜"-wide) pregathered lace
1 yd. (¼"-wide) ribbon
3 yds. (1"-wide) bias tape
1 yd. (2-3 mm.) braided macramé cord
2 (10 mm.) wooden beads
thread to match

From the quilted fabric, cut one bottom, one top, and one 7"-diameter circle according to patterns. Cut two (3½" x 14½") strips from same fabric.

To make each handle, fold one strip lengthwise with right sides together and sew a seam ¼" from long raw edge. Turn strip right side out and press with seam down center. Cut two 14½"-long pieces of lace; pin both pieces to handle so that pregathered edges overlap each other along center line. Sew in place with zigzag stitch. Cut one 14½" length of ribbon and pin along center of the handle so that ribbon hides stitching. Sew along each side of ribbon. Repeat for other handle.

Cut along fold line of top pattern piece (you should have two "C"-shaped pieces). Sew bias tape to cover all straight edges, leaving ends unfinished. Sew more bias tape to cover inner edges, turning under ends for smooth finish. Set top pieces aside.

To make the padded bottom, sew bias tape around edge of 7" circle. Pin this circle to center of larger circle with wrong sides together; then stitch two pieces together along both inner and outer edges of bias tape.

Pin top and bottom pieces together with right sides out. You will be able to see right side of the 7" circle through opening in center. Pin two handles on top as indicated, pulling handles tight and trimming ends where they extend over edge. Sew bias tape around circle to cover all raw edges.

Thread macramé cord through bias tape around center, leaving about 4" at each end. Trim ends of cord with wooden beads; then tie knot above and below beads to hold.★

A PILLOW FOR ALL SEASONS

Here is a year-round pillow with a Christmas twist. A traditional basket design, based on an old quilt pattern, is decorated with French knots done in candlewicking thread. The basket is sewn to the front of a muslin pillow trimmed with a wide lace ruffle. The top of the basket is left open so that you may fill it with silk poinsettias during the holidays. At other times of the year, change to daisies, tulips, violets, or whatever colorful blossoms you prefer, with a ribbon to match.

YOU WILL NEED:
pattern on page 150
½ yd. unbleached muslin
embroidery floss to match muslin
candlewicking thread (natural)
1 yd. muslin piping
2 yds. each red and green piping
2 yds. (4"-wide) pregathered lace
pillow form (16"-square)
⅔ yd. (⅜"-wide) ribbon

All embroidery using floss is worked with three strands in needle. The candlewicking (French knots) is worked with all four strands. Use purchased piping, or make your own by using a zipper foot to cover a cord with a strip of fabric cut on the bias.

Transfer design for bottom of basket to a 10" square of muslin. Using floss, embroider straight lines in outline stitch to form triangles. Switch to candlewicking thread and fill in alternate triangles with randomly spaced French knots (see pattern and photograph). Trim around basket, leaving ⅜" seam allowance. Sew row of muslin piping around this edge. Cut another 10" square of muslin. Place embroidered basket face-down on this square and sew through both layers, following sewing line of piping and leaving small opening at bottom for turning. Trim away excess fabric, clip curves, and turn. Whipstitch opening closed.

Cut two 17" x 17" squares from muslin. Pin basket to right side of one square and sew around sides and bottom, leaving top edge of basket free. Transfer design for handle to muslin square above basket. Satin stitch handle with floss, alternating direction of your stitches (see pattern). Make two small buttonholes at base of one side of handle.

This pillow has a double row of piping in different colors, but you may also make it with a single row, leaving off one of the colors. Sew red piping around outside edge of pillow front with raw edges touching (use a ½" seam allowance). Then sew green piping very close to red. Following same stitching line, sew a row of pregathered lace around edge, with ruffle turned toward inside of pillow.

Pin front to back with right sides facing. Again following same line of stitching, sew together, leaving an opening large enough for inserting pillow form. Turn pillow, insert form, and whipstitch opening closed. Thread ribbon through buttonholes and tie in bow. Fill basket with a few sprays of silk poinsettias or other flowers.★

A GIFT FROM NEPTUNE

Gleaming with the translucent beauty that only the sea can give, this ornament is the perfect way to use last summer's shells. If most of your own shells are small, then start with a larger, purchased shell such as the Mexican Flat Natural shown here.

Using either quick-drying white household glue or a hot glue gun, attach several sprigs of artificial or preserved cedar at the top. Add a bow made of double-faced satin ribbon. Arrange a few shells artistically and glue in place. Add a loop of golden cord.★

CURLY-TOPPED ANGELS

Flights of angels grace this tree sprinkled with stars—and at the very top is a sweet-faced angel treetopper that doubles as a doll when the holidays are over. The doll's legs are hidden, when she is an angel on the tree, by her eyelet dress with ruffly lace trim.

The angel ornaments are easy to make from bits and pieces of fabric you probably have on hand. Trim them with a variety of laces so that each will be slightly different. To complement the angels, hang an array of twinkly star ornaments. Even a child can make these—simply buy a box of gummed stars (from an office supply or art store) and stick two together back to back with a loop of gold thread between.

ANGEL DOLL:
patterns on pages 132 and 133
¼ yd. (45″-wide) fabric (for body, arms, legs, wings, and slip)
1 yd. (8″-wide) eyelet fabric with finished edge (for dress)
6″ x 8″ quilt batting
polyester stuffing
embroidery floss (black and pink)
2-ply sport yarn (for hair)
1½ yds. (1½″-wide) pregathered lace
heavy-duty thread or crochet cotton
½ yd. (¼″-wide) satin ribbon

Cut 2 bodies, 4 arms, 4 legs, 2 wings and a slip (6¾″ x 22″) from white fabric. Cut a skirt (7½″ x 22″) and 2 sleeves (4″ x 6″) from eyelet fabric with long edge of both skirt and sleeves along finished edge of eyelet. Cut one wing from batting. Set all pieces aside.

Allow a ¼″ seam allowance around all pattern pieces when making doll. Place front and back of body with right sides together and sew, leaving bottom open. Clip seam allowance at neck and turn right sides out. Embroider facial features with two strands of floss: eyes and eyebrows are done in black backstitch; mouth is done in pink straight stitch. Turn under ¼″ at bottom of body; press.

Make each arm by sewing a front to back, right sides facing. Turn, stuff firmly, and set aside. Make two legs in same manner.

Tuck ends of legs inside body; sew, catching only back of body and top of legs. Stuff body and head; whipstitch front to back.

To make hair, wrap yarn around narrow side of a 1½″ x 12″ strip of heavy paper. Stitch lengthwise down center of paper, catching loops of yarn (figure 1). Tear away paper from beneath, leaving only yarn. Sew hair onto head by hand. Begin by sewing curve of hair to back of head; sew hair from side seam over top to other side (figure 2).

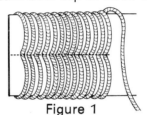

Figure 1   Figure 2

DRESS: Sew narrow ends of skirt together, right sides facing, to form back seam. Repeat step for slip. Place skirt over slip so that right side of each faces up and top raw edges are aligned. Sew skirt and slip together along top edge. Turn up bottom of slip ¼″; sew two rows of lace around edge to cover hem. Press crease in skirt so that bottom of skirt ends where lace on slip begins.

Fold each sleeve with right sides facing and sew underarm seam; turn right side out. Insert an arm in each sleeve and stitch across top, catching arm inside. Pin one sleeve to each side of dress at neck; then stitch together along top. Gather neck of dress with heavy thread (by hand) and catch at neck of doll to hold. Sew ends of 8″-long piece of lace together and gather with heavy thread around neck to form collar. Lace will hide rough edges of arms. Tie bow with narrow satin ribbon and tack to front of neck.

Place two wings with right sides together; then place batting on top. Sew through all three layers, leaving an opening to turn. Trim batting close to seam and clip seam allowances around curves. Turn, press, and sew opening closed. Quilt by hand or machine, if desired. Tack wings to "X" on back.

ANGEL ORNAMENT (to make one):

patterns on pages 132 and 133
remnant of fabric (for body)
6″ x 12″ white fabric (for wings)
6″ x 6″ quilt batting
3½″ x 15″ small print fabric (for dress)
polyester stuffing
embroidery floss (red and black)
2-ply sport yarn (for hair)
15″ (1″-wide) lace
heavy-duty thread or crochet cotton
8″ (1½″-wide) pregathered lace or fabric
  edged with lace

Cut a front and back body from body fabric, 2 wings from white fabric, 1 wing from quilt batting, and 1 rectangle (3½″ x 15″) from dress fabric. Set aside.

Use ¼″ seam allowance around all pattern pieces when making ornament. Sew front and back of body together, right sides facing, leaving opening on side. Turn right sides out, stuff, and close. Using black floss, embroider eyes in flystitch and eyebrows in straight stitch. Embroider red mouth in straight stitch. Add hair (see page 67).

Turn under ⅛″ on long edge of dress fabric; sew 1″-wide lace to cover this edge. Sew back of dress together with right sides facing. Turn dress right side out and press ¼″ toward inside along top edge. Gather top edge with heavy thread, drawing it up to fit around neck and tacking it in place. Sew ends of wider lace together, gather around neck in same manner, and attach to back. Trim dress with a bow of narrow ribbon or crochet cotton.

Make wings as directed for wings on the angel doll. Attach wings to back and add a loop of thread for hanging.★

A TISKET, A TASKET

Turn an old basket into a clever holder for rolls, your sewing, or almost anything else you need to carry from place to place. Trim the bottom with puffy gathered fabric; then add a lid with a cross-stitched "Country Christmas" duck design.

Because the size of the basket may vary so much, no quantities are given for the materials you will need. The duck motif for the lid is adaptable to many different sizes but will work best on a basket larger than six inches across at the top.

YOU WILL NEED:
chart and color key on page 147
purchased basket
matboard
#14 Aida cloth (blue)
mini-print fabric
embroidery floss (in colors shown in
  color key)
polyester batting
white household glue
contrasting piping
ribbon (⅜"-wide)
polyester stuffing
cord or string

Cut piece of matboard to fit inside basket just beneath rim. Using matboard as pattern, lightly pencil a line on Aida cloth and lining; add ½" seam allowance. Staystitch and cut.

Center design on Aida cloth; work according to chart. Outline all colors with one strand of black floss in backstitch.

Sew piping around embroidered top, aligning raw edges and using penciled line for stitching guide. Cut batting same shape as matboard and glue together. Place matboard on wrong side of embroidery, batting side down. Place lining, right side up, on top of both, keeping design centered. Turn raw edges of lining, piping, and Aida cloth under and pin in place. Whipstitch around edge, catching two ribbon-loop handles at sides.

Measure height of basket and also distance around widest part. Add 4" to height; then double the distance around. Cut strip of fabric to these measurements. Turn under 1½" along one long edge (top) and press. Make two rows of machine stitching ¾" and 1¼" from folded edge. Turn under 1" along other long edge (bottom) and press. Stitch ½" from folded edge. Seam short ends together, leaving openings at ½"-wide top and bottom casings.

Insert ribbon through casing at top of fabric, using enough ribbon to go around basket and still make a bow. Thread cord through casing at bottom. Wrap outside of basket with polyester stuffing to give a soft, full appearance. Insert basket in fabric cover, drawing cover up to fit. Adjust ribbon around top first; then pull cord at bottom to fit snugly. Hide end of cord and tie ribbon in a bow.★

NO BIGGER THAN A WALNUT

Charming on the tree, delightful when used as favors—these delicately detailed miniatures are made from bread dough and walnuts! Each ornament begins as a whole walnut, shown here larger than life-size. The walnut is cut to shape and decorated with figures and holly leaves molded from a special mixture of dough. The finished ornament is painted and varnished to a high gloss.

YOU WILL NEED:
bread dough (recipe follows)
acrylic paint
English walnuts
small hobby saw or hobby motor tool
  with radial saw blade attachment
small tools for making details (toothpicks,
  plastic drinking straws, ceramic cleaning
  tools, manicure tools, etc.)
white household glue
acrylic polymer varnish (Ceramcoat®)
metallic cord
wood craft sticks and small wood block
  (for baby carriage)
stain (for baby carriage)
small jewelry ring (for angel halo)

BREAD DOUGH:
3 slices white bread
3 tablespoons white household glue
3 drops glycerin (obtain at drugstores)
3 drops lemon juice
acrylic paint (red, green, and white)

Prepare dough by removing crusts and tearing bread into small crumbs. Add glue, glycerin, and lemon juice, mixing until a soft ball forms. Knead mixture with your hands until a very smooth dough is obtained. Divide dough into 3 parts, tinting each part with one drop of red, green, or white acrylic paint. (Tinting dough makes it much easier to hide any spots that you miss when you paint figures.) Store bread dough in small plastic bags until ready to use.

Most craft stores carry a selection of small motorized hobby tools with interchangeable grinding surfaces or saw blades. These are extremely useful in any craft requiring precision cutting on fragile or brittle materials, such as nut shells. Unless you are making an ornament using exactly half of the walnut, you will need to cut the shell to the proper shape with one of these tools.

To make ornaments with a closed back, cut horizontally across one side of shell first; then cut vertically along natural seam of shell until you reach first cut. Make basket-type ornament in the same manner, but instead of following natural seam for vertical cut, make a cut about ⅛" to each side of the seam to form a handle. Make round hole in birdhouse ornament with a drill; then enlarge hole with a grinder. After making your cuts, remove all nut meat with a pick and grind down any rough spots inside the shell.

Use the photographs on these pages as a guide when making your ornaments, or let them serve as inspiration for your own ideas. Begin by filling bottom of empty shell with a small piece of dough, pressing it into shell with your fingers. As a rule, it is best to make main figure first; then add leaves and berries as trimming to hide rough edges. Make figures by shaping and rolling round and oval pieces of dough, using the color of dough which most closely matches finished color. To attach figures and leaves to each other or base, dab a bit of slightly diluted glue on both the surfaces. Make tiny details by pressing dough with a toothpick.

Make holly leaves by flattening a ball of dough and using a plastic drinking straw to cut edges in a scalloped shape. Make veins in leaves with a sharp tool; holly berries are tiny balls of dough.

Glue a loop of metallic cord to top of shell if you are making a hanging ornament. If you prefer a tabletop ornament, place a ball of dough under shell and hide edges with holly leaves.

Allow at least 24 hours for dough to dry completely. Paint in bright colors with acrylic paint; then seal ornament with two coats of glossy varnish.

The baby stroller ornament requires some simple woodcarving with a very sharp craft knife. Make base from a 1" x 1" x ½" block of soft wood, carving an indentation in top of block to fit bottom curve of walnut shell. Shape thin, soft wood or craft sticks for the sides of the stroller (see photograph); then drill a hole in the end of each side, insert a length of toothpick to act as a handle, and glue sides to block of wood. Cut thin slices from a small diameter dowel for wheels, drill a hole in center of each, and insert small pieces of toothpick to peg wheels to the base. Stain and varnish stroller before gluing finished walnut shell in place.★

LUCY LAMBCHOP

Dressed in her Christmas finery, this little girl lamb does everything but bat her eyes to make sure she is noticed on the tree. Her body is made of fluffy fur fabric, and her arms and legs are shaped from rolls of felt. Just a bit of simple sewing is required to put her together in time for the holidays.

YOU WILL NEED:
patterns on page 137
scrap of "lambswool" fabric
scrap of felt (gray, beige, or light brown)
polyester stuffing
white household glue
6" each (⅛"-and ½"-wide) ribbon
small bell
2 black beads (for eyes)
black embroidery floss
rhinestone or small flower
6" gold thread (for hanging)

Cut 1 body from fur fabric. Cut 4 arm/leg pieces, 2 heads, and 1 tail from felt. Sew body along side seams, with right sides together, leaving a small opening for stuffing. Turn right side out, stuff, and sew closed.

To make arms and legs, roll each piece of felt tightly beginning at *long* side; glue along edge and hold with pins until glue dries. Whipstitch end of one arm to each side of body. Tack both arms to body on front, add bow made of narrow ribbon, and trim with bell. Attach legs to body as shown; then slit ⅛" up front of each leg to form a hoof.

Sew around edge of both head pieces with ⅛" seam, leaving a small opening for stuffing—seam allowance will be on the *outside*. Sew on beads for eyes and make mouth and nose with 6 strands of embroidery floss (see photograph). Use pencil to push stuffing into head but not ears; then sew seam closed. Tack the head firmly to body.

Make bow from ½"-wide ribbon, sew it to head, and add rhinestone or flower. Glue tail to middle of back. Make loop for hanging from metallic thread.★

MERRY MERRY MOOSE

Wide-eyed and woolly, this moose with the bemused expression is sure to bring smiles to your friends. Because it works up very quickly and requires a minimum of sewing, this fur and felt ornament is a good last-minute gift for a neighbor or someone you almost forgot!

YOU WILL NEED:
patterns on page 137
scrap of dark brown shag fur fabric
scraps of felt (beige and brown)
polyester stuffing
white household glue
2 (¼"-wide) wiggly eyes (purchased)
red pom-pom (½"-wide)
16" (⅛"-wide) ribbon
small bell

Cut 1 body from fur fabric. Cut 2 heads, 4 legs, and 1 double-ear piece from beige felt. Cut 2 antlers from brown felt.

Fold body with right sides together. Sew side seams; turn right sides out, stuff, and whipstitch bottom opening closed.

Spread glue on one side of each felt strip. Beginning at a short edge, tightly roll each strip to form a leg. Glue all four legs together and glue to bottom of body.

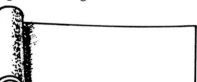

Whipstitch around head to join both pieces, leaving top open between two dots; stuff. Whipstitch antlers together around edges, leaving opening at bottom. Push stuffing into antlers; sew closed. Fold ears lengthwise, matching dots; whipstitch center together so that ears cup.

Sew top of head closed; tack on ears and antlers. Sew head to body. Glue bit of fur at forehead. Glue on eyes and a pom-pom nose; trim with bow and bell. Add loop.★

GIDDYUP REINDEER

A playful reindeer riding toy under the tree on Christmas morning will delight any young child. And having a *pair* of them means that your child and a little friend can romp and gallop to their hearts' content—outside, of course!

Each reindeer has a head made from a sock, while the expressive facial features are embroidered with floss. Colorful buttons, bows, and holiday hats make these lovable characters the best-dressed twosome in town.

YOU WILL NEED (for one riding toy):
patterns on pages 134 and 135
one Rockford Red Heel® sock (medium)
¼ yd. fabric (for antlers)
scrap of pink felt (for ears)
extra sock fabric (optional, for ears)
polyester stuffing
embroidery floss (black, brown, white,
  and red)
36" (¾"-diameter) wooden dowel
small amount white yarn
two (¾"-long) brads or nails
specific materials listed below

GIRL:
one pair craft eyelashes (purchased)
3 yds. (⅞"-wide) red ribbon
2 green buttons

BOY:
remnant of red velvet or flannel (for hat)
⅛ yd. white "lambswool" fabric
1½ yds. (⅞"-wide) green ribbon
2 red buttons

Cut four antlers from antler fabric. For each antler, place two pieces with right sides facing and sew around seam allowance. Clip almost to seam line around all curves, turn, and stuff, pushing the stuffing in with the end of a pencil.

Cut two ears from pink felt and two ears from either an extra sock or fabric. Sew a felt and fabric ear together, right sides facing. Turn; repeat for other ear.

Stuff sock, leaving four inches of cuff empty. Hold temporarily with a rubber band. Whipstitch one ear to each side of red heel, hiding rough edges by turning them to inside (see photographs for placement). Turn under raw edges of antlers and pin in place slightly closer to center and just in front of red heel. Whipstitch around base to hold.

The position of features on face determines individual expression of reindeer. Draw features with a pencil and embroider with six strands of floss. (Eyes, noses, and girl's mouth are worked in satin stitch, while boy's mouth is worked in large backstitch.) If you are making girl, take a long stitch through two dots on pattern and pull together to form a "puckered-up-for-a-kiss" mouth. Using black thread, whipstitch base of eyelashes over eyes for girl.

Remove rubber band and insert one end of dowel into sock, with end of dowel almost reaching heel. Form a small loop of white yarn; holding loop up with end sticking down about four inches, *tightly* wrap yarn about fifty times around both dowel and sock. Cut yarn, insert cut end through loop, and pull first end of yarn down *hard* to secure loop beneath wraps. Trim excess yarn. Nail two small brads into stick through yarn.

Make bridle by wrapping 9 inches of ribbon around nose to fit; pin with ends slightly overlapping. Pin one end of a 40"-long piece of ribbon at each side, turn under, and tack in place, covering stitches with buttons. For girl, make a bow from 12 inches of ribbon and tack in front of antlers. Tie remaining ribbon in a bow around neck; stitch.

If making boy, cut hat from red velvet and hatband from fur fabric. Stitch hatband to bottom of hat; sew hat together along back seam with right sides facing. Turn right side out; cut two slits for antlers and ears.★

DECK THE HALLS

Stretched across the mantel, framing the top of the door, or swagged on the staircase, this plump holly garland lends a bright and festive touch to holiday decorating. Besides its many traditional uses, the middle section of this versatile garland even acts as a low centerpiece when stretched down the middle of the table—it's especially attractive if you tuck in some short, fat candles to add extra glow.

Use basic "stitch and stuff" techniques for each of the leaves, berries, and candy canes. Tack the separate elements together to form the garland; then add a bow to each end.

YOU WILL NEED:
patterns on page 136
1⅔ yds. (45"-wide) green calico fabric
1 yd. (45"-wide) red fabric
¼ yd. (45"-wide) red/white striped fabric
thread to match
polyester stuffing
3 (1"-diameter) plastic rings.

From the green calico, cut fronts and backs for 24 holly leaves (this will be a total of 48 pieces). From the red fabric, cut two strips, each 12" wide by 45" long, for the bows. Cut 10 circles for berries from the remaining red fabric. Place the pattern for the candy cane diagonally on the striped fabric, and cut 2 canes (there will be a total of 4 pieces).

HOLLY LEAF (make 24): Stitch two pieces, right sides together, with a ¼" seam, leaving an opening for turning. Clip the curves; then turn right side out. Fill with polyester stuffing and sew opening closed. Stitch along the center of each leaf with the sewing machine to form a vein.

BERRY (make 10): Baste around each circle by hand, ¼" from the edge. With the wrong side toward you, pull gently at the threads so that the fabric forms a pouch. Stuff firmly and continue pulling thread until the pouch closes. Tack with several stitches.

CANE (make 2): Matching the stripes as closely as possible, sew two cane pieces, right sides together and ¼" from the edge; leave open at each end. Clip the curves, turn right side out, and stuff firmly. Baste by hand around both ends with long running stitches, ¼" from the edge. Pull tightly to close, and tack in place to secure.

BOW (make 2): Fold each strip of red fabric lengthwise with right sides together, and stitch along the long edge, leaving 6" in the center open. Pin with the seam at the back center. Sew an inverted "V" at each end. Trim away extra fabric, turn right side out, and make sure that the points are turned well. Press.

ASSEMBLY: Tack three leaves together to form one unit (see diagram for placement); continue until 18 leaves are used. Tack two of these bunches together to form the 6-leaved center section. Working outward from the center, whipstitch two more 3-leaved units to each side, slightly overlapping the point of the previous unit to cover the base of the next. Sew remaining leaves at ends.

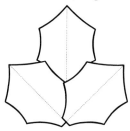

Tack a candy cane to each end, slanting both canes toward the center. Attach the bases of the last two leaf units to the bottom of the candy canes. Tack four holly berries securely to the middle of the center section; then tack one berry to the center of each remaining unit.

Tie a fluffy bow with each of the red strips; tack one bow to the front of each candy cane. Sew a hanging ring to the back of the center and at each end—the placement of the rings may vary, depending on how you wish the garland to hang.★

GOODY BAGS

For wrapping festive foods, bottled beverages, puzzle pieces, mounds of marbles, or anything else that is unusual in shape, a bag may be better than a box! These bags are quick to make and offer a chance to use the lovely Christmas-print fabrics available this time of year. It is best to place food gifts, such as the Quick Mix for pancakes and muffins shown here (recipe on page 105) in plastic zip-type bags inside the fabric bags.

YOU WILL NEED (to make three bags):
1 yd. plus 2" (44"-wide) fabric
2 yds. (⅜"-wide) ribbon for trim
5¼ yds. (1"-wide) ribbon
thread to match

Cut two rectangles (16" by 9½") for front and back of each bag. Sew a double row of ⅜"-wide ribbon trim to narrow end of front rectangle, placing rows 6" and 7" from top raw edge. Pin front and back with right sides facing, and stitch around sides and bottom using a ⅝" seam. Turn.

Turn under 2 inches around top edge of bag; press. Make channel around top by sewing two parallel rows of zigzag stitching 1" and 1¾" from top fold. Using small, sharp scissors, cut a slit through only top layer of fabric at each side seam (between two zigzagged rows). Cut two 22" lengths of 1"-wide ribbon; thread through channels.★

STITCH UP A STOCKING

A reindeer on rockers decorates this stocking, which is roomy enough to please even the most hopeful child! Because the design is created with simple machine-appliqué techniques, you will enjoy making it as much as your child will enjoy using it. Two construction methods are given—one for woven fabrics and one for felt—so whether your taste runs to traditional calico or wildly colorful fabrics, you can make the stocking to suit your home.

YOU WILL NEED:
patterns on pages 142 and 143
⅜ yd. iron-on interfacing
thread to match appliqué pieces
embroidery floss for eye
⅜ yd. cotton fabric (for lining)
¼ yd. (½"-wide) ribbon
specific materials listed below

FELT STOCKING:
⅜ yd. pink felt
9" x 12" felt squares in bright green, hot
   pink, orange, and red
felt scraps in green, yellow, purple, blue,
   and light orange
⅝ yd. Stitch Witchery® fusible fabric bond

CALICO STOCKING:
⅜ yd. light blue cotton fabric
scraps of cotton mini-print fabric in the
   following colors: green (2 prints), red (2
   prints), brown, dark brown, and yellow

Fuse iron-on interfacing to back of each piece of fabric that will become an appliqué, fusing only enough to accommodate pattern pieces that will be cut from each color. (Do *not* fuse interfacing to fabric for stocking body.) Transfer patterns for appliqués to desired color of felt or calico; then cut pieces with very sharp scissors. Machine appliqué each piece in position, using a closely-spaced, medium-width zigzag stitch.

Using a ¼" seam allowance, sew both top section and toe section to center front. Press

seams open. Repeat for the back of the stocking. Embroider a backstitched eye on reindeer, using three strands of floss. Cut a front and back from lining fabric, following completed stocking front as a pattern.

Instructions for the two stockings will now be different. If you are making the felt stocking, cut two pieces of Stitch Witchery® to same size as lining. Fuse both front and back to their respective linings with wrong sides together. Cut a 5" length of ribbon, double it to form a loop, and pin it to top right side of stocking front. Stitch across top of front and then top of back, ¼" inside edge. Pin front and back together with linings facing; then stitch through all four layers ¼" from edge. Trim neatly with pinking shears.

If you are making the calico stocking, sew front and back, with right sides together, around all sides except top, using a ¼" seam. Sew two lining pieces together in same manner. Turn stocking right side out; press. Insert lining in stocking. Turn under top edge of each approximately ⅜", press, and whipstitch together, catching a doubled 5" length of ribbon on right side as you go. You may wish to reinforce base of hanging loop with machine stitching for extra strength.★

FAR EASTERN ORNAMENTS

Shimmering like magical spheres from exotic regions of the world, these ornaments are made with silky flosses and metallic threads. Although the technique is based on that used for traditional Japanese *Temari* balls, it has been greatly simplified without sacrificing the intricate overlay of color and pattern that gives these ornaments their unique beauty.

Each of the ornaments you make will be one-of-a-kind and the design will vary from ball to ball. As long as you follow the basic process outlined below, beginning with sectioning the ball, you can add layer after layer of color and pattern until you are pleased with the results.

YOU WILL NEED:
plastic foam balls (about 3"-diameter)
sewing thread (one spool per ball)
glass-head pins
metallic thread (gold or silver)
silky rayon floss (or perle cotton)
blunt needle

Wrap plastic foam ball with sewing thread until ball is completely covered with a network of criss-crossed threads. Mark with a pin at exact top and bottom.

Use metallic thread to divide ball into halves from top to bottom, winding thread once around each pin to hold it in place. Divide in half again to make four sections; then repeat to make a total of eight equal vertical sections (figure 1). The ball will now be sectioned like an orange.

Anchor top by weaving silky floss like a spiderweb around spokes of metallic thread, looping floss around each time you cross the spoke (figure 2). Continue weaving until you have come about ¼" out from center pin. Repeat to anchor bottom; remove pins.

To understand the basic principle for making these ornaments, look at the peach, green, and gold ornament in the photograph. Notice the gold threads making a zigzag pattern around the middle. This pattern is formed by single threads which go around the ball but are pulled through the base layer of thread in a consistent *up and down* pattern divided according to sections.

The green zigzag pattern above the gold pattern is made the same way, at slightly different angles, yet still according to sections. A second green zigzag pattern is overlaid on the first to create diamonds. Use one section, two sections, or even half of a section at a time to make the design, *as long as you are consistent in going around the entire ball.*

Begin your design by going around middle in a zigzag pattern with floss or metallic thread. (Mark your place with pins all around the ball before you begin, to keep pattern even.) As you make zigzag, catch needle through base layer of thread whenever you change directions or cross a thread that divides ball into sections. Repeat until you have six or eight strands making same pattern.

Begin new series of zigzags, using either same color of floss or different color. Second zigzag may overlap first or not, as you wish. Continue process of making new rings of zigzags, working from middle toward top; then repeat process to make patterns on bottom. An intricate design will evolve as you work.

If you wrap several strands of floss when you cross dividing threads, as shown in figure 2, a ridge will result. If you do not wrap floss, but merely catch it in the layer of thread below, a smooth finish will result. When ball is covered with a pattern of zigzags, make a thread loop through top.★

Figure 1

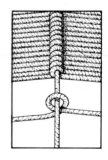

Figure 2

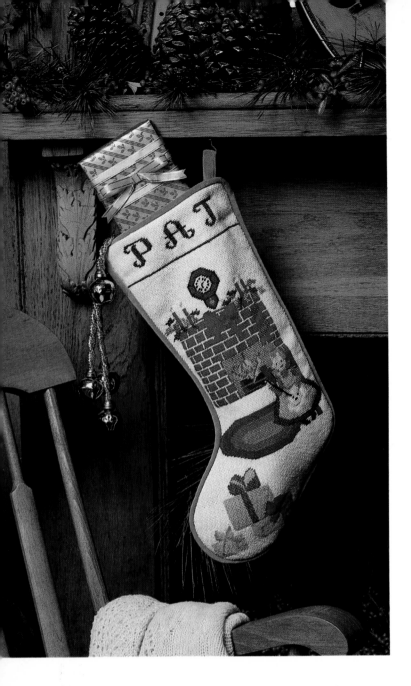

A NEEDLEWORKER'S STOCKING

If your greatest pleasure comes from creating beautiful needlework for your family and friends, then this is a project you'll enjoy. The personalized stocking shows a contented lady sitting in front of the fire doing exactly what you're doing—needlepoint.

A backing of velvet lends elegance and durability to this heirloom-quality stocking. In years to come, the cozy scene on the front will remind you of the hours you spent so pleasantly while making it.

YOU WILL NEED:
pattern and charts on pages 124 and
  148-149
#14 mesh mono interlocked canvas
  (14" x 22")
3-ply Persian yarn in colors shown on
  color key on page 148
½ yd. cotton velvet fabric for backing
1⅓ yds. cording
½ yd. white lining fabric

Trace outline of the stocking onto canvas with hard pencil or needlepoint marker. Work needlepoint motifs from chart, spacing them on stocking as shown in photograph and leaving room at top for a name or initials. Chart initials on graph paper first; then find center of your chart in order to center letters on canvas. Work letters. Fill in background last. Block needlepoint and allow to dry thoroughly. Trim excess canvas, leaving ⅝" seam allowance around outline.

Use purchased cording or make your own. To make cording, cut 2½"-wide bias strips from velvet and wrap, with wrong sides together, around cable cord. Machine stitch with zipper foot along side of cord. Trim seam allowance to ⅝" if necessary. Align raw edges of cording with raw edge of stocking front, right sides together, and stitch around all edges.

Cut a rectangle (14" x 22") from velvet, but do *not* cut according to stocking pattern. Place stocking front over velvet rectangle, right sides together, and pin in place with pins on front. Machine stitch around all sides except top (use previous row of stitching as your guide). Clip fabric at curves and trim away excess fabric. Turn right side out.

Using pattern, make lining, adding ⅝" seam allowance all around. Cut strip of velvet (3" x 16¾"). Allowing ⅝" seam, stitch strip to top edge of completed lining, right sides together; then stitch ends closed. Slip lining inside finished stocking. Turn top edge of strip of velvet to inside so that it covers both edge of cording on front and raw edge on back. Whipstitch to close. Make loop from scrap of velvet and stitch to top.★

SOMETHING FOR THE KIDS

Basic crochet stitches and scraps of yarn are all that are needed to make these cuddly critters. Imagine the mouse peering out of a stocking on Christmas morning, or the bear tucked into a toddler's pocket!

Both animals may be used as "extra" gifts to tie on a package or as appliqués to sew on a sweater if you crochet just the front layer. To make a larger version, add a crocheted back and stuff between the layers for a soft, safe toy.

YOU WILL NEED:
1 oz. each of Pingouin Le Yarn #28 brown (MC) and #57 light brown (CC) for bear
1 oz. each of Pingouin Le yarn #21 gray (MC) and #54 pink (CC) for mouse
small amounts of black, red, white, and pink yarn (for details)
crochet hook size H
yarn needle
polyester stuffing (for larger toy)

BODY: With CC, ch 4. Join with sl st to form ring. *Round 1:* Sc over ring 12 times and join tog with sl st. *Round 2:* Work 1 dc through both loops of first sc, then 2 dc in next st. Alternate 1 dc and 2 dc around. Join with sl st. *Round 3:* Break off CC and attach MC and repeat Round 2. (For larger stuffed toy, add *Round 4:* Work 2 dc in each st around.)

PAWS: With MC, work 1 dc in each of 4 sts. Turn, ch 2, repeat dc to end. Skipping 3 sts in between, repeat for remaining 3 paws. There will be wide space left for attaching neck. (For larger toy, work 1 additional row of dc for paws. Skip 8 sts between paws.)

HEAD: For Bear: Work as for body, omitting paws. For Mouse: Work Round 1 in CC. Change to MC for Rounds 2 and 3. (For larger toy, work Round 4.) Attach head to neck with sl st.

EARS: For Bear, attach MC in 3rd st from center of top of head. Ch 4, join with sl st to same st. Turn and work 9 dc over ch. Secure to head with sl st. Repeat for other ear.

For Mouse, attach CC in 3rd st from center of top of head. Ch 4, join with sl st to same st. Turn and work 7 dc over ch. Break off CC, attach MC and, working on right side, dc in each dc around. Secure through original st. Ears will cup. (For larger toy, work additional row of dc.)

FINISHING: Use yarn needle and bits of scrap yarn to embroider eyes, nose, mouth, or tongue in satin stitch and backstitch (see photograph). For Mouse, add whiskers; make tail by attaching double strand of MC and working ch as long as desired. Fasten off.

For larger toy: Work back same as front using MC only. Work satin stitch over centers of tummy, back, and back of head. Join front to back using MC and sl st all around, leaving space open to stuff. Stuff lightly with polyester. Close opening with sl st and sew tail to mouse.★

Standard Crochet Abbreviations

st(s) - stitch(es)	**sl st** - slip stitch
ch(s) - chain(s)	**MC** - main color
sc - single crochet	**CC** - contrasting color
dc - double crochet	**tog** - together

#5 millinery needle
matboard (4" x 4")
green fabric (5" x 5" for backing)
white household glue
gold foil paper (4" x 4")
⅓ yd. (⅛"-wide) satin ribbon

Lightly mark Congress cloth with main elements on pattern, using sharp pencil. Turn under edges of cloth so that approximately 5 threads are toward back on all sides. Leaving two threads on front edges bare, work green stem stitch around square, going through both layers of cloth to hold turned-under portion in place. Beginning 6 threads down from stem stitch and 14 threads from corner stem stitch, embroider row of green coral knot stitch indicated in long broken lines. Repeat on all four sides.

The tree is completely covered in cast-on buttonhole stitch—cast 6 stitches on needle at the top and 8 at bottom. Begin at top of tree and make random stitches in direction that branches would grow. (Marks on outline of tree in pattern indicate extensions of branches.)

Using red floss, scatter a few French knots over tree; make tree trunk with bullion knot stitches. (9 wraps at top, 6 at bottom). Still using red floss, make triple lazy daisy with bullion knot (4 wraps) at each corner. Make row of Y-stitches (6 threads wide and 4 threads deep) between rows of green, repeating along each side.

Change to gold thread and make star at top of tree (8 French knots on stems radiating from center). Make more French knots and knots on stems at each corner.

ASSEMBLY: Glue green fabric to matboard, with raw edges glued on other side. Sandwich gold foil (shiny side up) between finished stitchery and fabric-covered matboard. Raw edges will be hidden between layers. Sew front and back together with blind stitch. Tie a ribbon bow and tack to top of plaque.★

A TINY CHRISTMAS TREE

This miniature plaque is a showcase for your finest embroidery skills. Worked in Brazilian embroidery on Congress cloth, the plaque is attractive displayed on an easel or even hanging on the tree.

If you have never before attempted to do Brazilian embroidery, study the stitch guide before beginning. You will see that most of the stitches are combinations of more familiar (and simple!) stitches.

YOU WILL NEED:
pattern on page 135
stitch guide on page 123
#24 white Congress cloth (4½" x 4½")
EDMAR "Lola"® rayon floss (217 green
  and 209 red)
gold metallic thread

A GINGERBREAD HOLIDAY

Gingerbread brings memories of long-ago Christmases—of wonderful fragrances and good times in the kitchen. You can't bring back those times, but you can make this cheerful wreath with its family of gingerbread boys. Made of wood, and painted in only two colors, it will last for years, until your children have memories of their own.

YOU WILL NEED:
patterns on pages 140 and 141
white pine shelving (10″ x 10″ x ¾″)
scraps of ¼″-thick plywood
band saw and drill
sandpaper
sealer
fruitwood stain
liquid acrylic paints (ivory and brown)
gold metallic cord
white household glue
saw-toothed hanger

Transfer pattern for wreath to pine shelving. Transfer patterns for bow and seven gingerbread boys to plywood. Cut with a band saw and sand all pieces; then seal wreath and bow only. Drill holes at top of two boys; stain all seven and allow to dry.

Paint wreath brown and add bands of ivory along edges. Dip end of a small brush in ivory and make dots on background. Paint bow with ivory, shading with brown (see photograph). Outline stained gingerbread boys with ivory and paint details.

Insert gold cord through holes in two gingerbread boys. Place ends on ''X'' at top of wreath, adjust to length desired, and apply glue to hold. Cover with bow, glue on remaining boys, and weight until glue dries. Nail saw-toothed hanger to back.★

A SLEIGH & A SKATER

A twinkle-toed skater glides beneath the branches of the tree, while on the table rests a sleigh loaded with colorful presents. Both ornaments are made of wood, painted very simply in acrylic paints with a minimum of shading. The paint is applied to all sides of the wood, including the edges. Use a good quality flat artist's brush for large areas of color and a very small brush for details.

YOU WILL NEED:
patterns on page 135
birch veneer plywood (¼"-thick)
scraps of wood (for sleigh)
jigsaw or band saw
sandpaper
sealer
white household glue (for sleigh)
acrylic paints
waterbase varnish
knitted doll's cap (purchased, for sleigh)

green, paint the mittens and make stripes on the scarf.

Use black paint on a tiny brush to make details (see photograph). Your own individual style will show in this step—different shading effects are determined by your brush technique and by how much you dilute the paint with water. Allow the paint to dry; then apply a coat of varnish. Drill a small hole at the top and attach a loop of gold metallic thread.

SLEIGH: Transfer all patterns to plywood and cut two sides, two ends, and one bottom. Cut a variety of small "packages" from scraps of wood and dowels (none should be over one cubic inch in size). Sand all pieces, seal, and allow to dry.

Draw the details on the sides of the sleigh with a sharp pencil. Glue both ends between the sides, following the guidelines on the diagram; then glue on the bottom. Paint a basecoat on the sleigh, inside and out, using two coats if necessary for good coverage. Paint details on the sleigh with red and black paint on a tiny, pointed brush.

Paint the packages in a variety of colors and use contrasting colors to make the ribbons. Glue packages in the sleigh in a pleasing arrangement. Apply varnish and allow to dry. Finish by gluing a small doll cap on one side of the sleigh.★

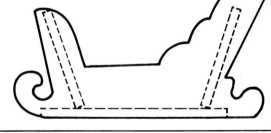

SKATER: Transfer the pattern to plywood and cut the outline with a jigsaw or band saw. Sand all edges smooth and seal, allowing to dry. Draw the details with pencil. Begin by painting the face and legs with flesh. Using red paint, fill in the coat and hat; then paint the mouth and, diluting the paint, color the cheeks. Paint the skates, buttons and scarf with white; then paint fur, using a stippling motion. Paint a brown base coat on the runners of the skates. With

Color Chart	
Skater:	**Sleigh:**
flesh	gold metallic
red	red
white	black
green	yellow
brown	green
black	blue

YOUR FAMILY TREE

Easy, inexpensive, yet as personal as a gift can be—this ornament is a family tree in the true sense of the word! Make one for your own family, of course; then make one for each of the families that you'd like to re-member with a small token this Christmas. Even a child can help with these.

To make baker's clay, mix 4 cups of all-purpose flour, 1 cup of salt, and 1¼ to 1½ cups of water. Knead mixture at least five minutes to develop gluten in flour and make a smooth dough. (Tint clay for the tree with green acrylic paint.) Roll on floured surface and cut tree and heart shapes with cookie cutters. Add hand-molded faces and hats, at-taching them to tree with a drop of water.

Insert a wire hanger at top of tree before baking. Bake on a cookie sheet in a 250° oven until hard (about 2½ hours). For rosy cheeks and bright colors on hats and hearts, paint cooled ornaments with acrylic paint. Dip into a can of glossy varnish four times, drying between coats. With a Sharpie® fine-tipped marking pen, add smiling faces and names of family members.★

88

CARDS TO KEEP

This year, send your nicest presents in an envelope! Cross-stitch one of these colorful designs in just an evening or two, mat it, and mail it—with a holiday message to your friends written on the back.

Take your choice of a bell, train, soldier, or perhaps a bear for baby's first Christmas. When the season is over, the card can be framed to display throughout the year.

YOU WILL NEED:
charts and color keys on pages 146 and 147
#14 Aida cloth (6" x 8" for bell, train, and soldier; 9" x 9" for bear)
embroidery floss (in colors indicated by color keys)
purchased cardboard mat for framing
white posterboard
Stitch Witchery® fusible fabric bond
white household glue

Using 3 strands of floss in colors suggested on chart, work the design in cross-stitch. Most craft stores and framing shops carry a wide selection of ready-made mats in a vari-ety of colors. Choose a mat with an opening which allows the whole design to show, yet still fits closely. A 5" x 7" mat with a 3" x 5" opening is fine for all designs except bear, which is shown in an 8"-square mat with a 5" circular opening.

Center cross-stitched cloth under mat; with pencil, draw around *outer* edge of mat. Cut Aida cloth to size about ¼" inside penciled line. Cut a piece of posterboard to exact outer dimensions of your mat. Cut piece of Stitch Witchery® 1" smaller in length and width.

Make a "sandwich" by placing wrong side of cloth facing wrong side of poster board, with piece of Stitch Witchery® between. Check placement of design by holding mat above, shifting everything until all layers are properly aligned. Remove mat, and press to fuse other layers together.

Run two thin lines of glue around under-side of mat, just inside inner and outer edges. Carefully place mat on top of mounted cross-stitch and weight with books until glue dries.

Write a holiday message on the back or glue on an actual Christmas card if you are sending one of these cards to a friend. If you are framing one for yourself, have a piece of glass cut to the same dimensions as the mat; this will protect the needlework from being damaged by dust.★

BAUBLES & BANGLES

A king's ransom in jewels? No—but these are undoubtedly the most opulent, glittery, utterly splendid ornaments you'll ever hang on your tree. Satin balls bedecked with rhinestones, pearls, and other costume jewelry hang from golden braid and velvet ribbons. The effect is dazzling, especially at night when the balls reflect the lights.

YOU WILL NEED:
satin-covered foam balls (not hollow)
costume jewelry
wire clippers
white household glue
1¼" straight pins
corsage pins with pearl or gold heads
velvet ribbons (a variety)
gold braid (a variety)

The more costume jewelry you add to these ornaments, the better they will look. The best places to find old jewelry, at giveaway prices, are rummage sales and garage sales. Don't worry about whether the earrings have backs (you will remove these anyway) or the necklaces have clasps (you will separate most of these into individual beads). Use wire clippers to break apart the jewelry.

Have a variety of ribbons and braids on hand. Imagination, and simple trial and error, are the keys to making these ornaments beautiful. Add and take away until you are pleased with the results.

Begin by dividing ball into quarters with ribbons and/or braids. Anchor ribbons with pins or with pins pushed through beads. Beginning at top, add earrings or beads to form a slightly raised crown. Glue in place and pin firmly with corsage pins. Add a loop of ribbon or braid for hanging, hiding glued ends as you add more jewelry.

Assemble jewelry for bottom—charm bracelets or beads on chains work best. Glue and pin in place. Working upwards, add more individual beads, earrings, or loops of beads to cover bare spaces. Symmetry is important for balance as well as appearance.★

THE SWEETS OF CHRISTMAS

> *STUFFED DATES*
> *CHOCOLATE SPIDERWEB SNAPS*
> *SLICE OF FRUIT COOKIES*
> *JAVA GEMS*
> *GLAZED SPICE BARS*
> *CREME DE CACAO BALLS*
> *ALMOND FUDGE RING*
> *YULE LOG*
> *AMBROSIA PIE*
> *SPECIAL CARROT CAKE*
> *APPLE-MINCE PIE*

Visions of sugarplums dance in the heads of most children and sometimes their parents, too, at Christmastime. Practically overnight, every table seems laden with sweets that appear only at this season. The choices are many—the cakes and cookies, the pies and candies, all those delectable goodies that tempt you to have "Well, just a small piece." You undoubtedly have some family favorites already, but the recipes given here might well become next year's choices by popular demand.

There's nothing like a good cookie to please a child, and these cookies are especially fun—the Slice of Fruit Cookies are shaped and flavored like lemons, limes and oranges, while the Chocolate Spiderweb Snaps have a layer of frosting to lick.

STUFFED DATES
1 (3-ounce) package cream cheese, softened
2 tablespoons powdered sugar
1 to 2 tablespoons orange juice
¼ cup chopped walnuts
1 (8-ounce) package pitted dates

Beat cream cheese until creamy. Add powdered sugar and enough orange juice to make a creamy stuffing consistency. Stir in walnuts. Make a lengthwise slit in dates. Stuff dates with cream cheese mixture. Yield: about 4 dozen.

CHOCOLATE SPIDERWEB SNAPS
4 (1-ounce) squares unsweetened chocolate
1¼ cups shortening
2 cups sugar
2 eggs
⅓ cup corn syrup
2½ tablespoons water
1 teaspoon vanilla extract
4 cups all-purpose flour
2 teaspoons baking soda
½ teaspoon salt
Frosting (recipe follows)
½ cup semisweet chocolate morsels

Melt unsweetened chocolate over hot water in top of double boiler. Remove from heat.

Cream shortening; gradually add sugar, beating until light and fluffy. Add melted chocolate, eggs, corn syrup, water, and vanilla; mix well. Combine flour, soda, and salt; add to creamed mixture, beating only until blended.

Shape dough into two long rolls, 2½ inches in diameter. Wrap in waxed paper and chill several hours. Unwrap rolls, and cut into ¼-inch slices. Place on ungreased cookie sheets; bake at 350° for 10 to 12 minutes. Cool on cookie sheets 5 minutes. Remove to wire racks, and cool completely. Spread frosting over cookies to within ⅛-inch of edge; let stand until frosting sets.

Melt chocolate morsels in top of double boiler; let stand until almost cool but not set. Spoon melted chocolate into decorating cone with metal tip No. 2 attached.

For round pattern, pipe chocolate in 5 or 6 circles around top of cookie. Pull the point of a wooden pick across chocolate circles from the center to the outer edge. Repeat this 8 or 10 times, spacing evenly across the top of cookie.

For linear pattern, pipe chocolate in parallel lines, about ¼-inch apart, across top of

---

Christmas confections come in all shapes and flavors: from right, Almond Fudge Ring, Chocolate Spiderweb Snaps, Glazed Spice Bars, Slice of Fruit Cookies, Java Gems.

Glazed Spice B
3/4 cup vegetable o
1/4 cup honey
_ cup sugar
_ all-purpose
_ on salt
_ n baking

cookie. Pull the point of a wooden pick diagonally across lines. Let stand at room temperature until chocolate is firm. Yield: 5 dozen.

Frosting:
6 cups powdered sugar
About 6 tablespoons warm water
Paste food coloring

Combine sugar and enough water to make frosting a spreading consistency, mixing well. Color as desired with a very small amount of paste food coloring. Yield: frosting for 5 dozen cookies.

SLICE OF FRUIT COOKIES
1 cup shortening
1½ cups sugar
2 eggs
1 teaspoon vanilla extract
3 tablespoons lemon juice
¼ cup plus 3 tablespoons orange juice
4½ cups all-purpose flour
½ teaspoon salt
Yellow, orange, and green paste food
  coloring
1½ teaspoons grated lemon rind
1½ teaspoons grated orange rind
1½ teaspoons grated lime rind
Yellow, orange, and green colored sugar
Royal Icing

Combine shortening and sugar, creaming until light and fluffy; stir in eggs, vanilla, and juices, mixing well. Combine flour and salt; add to creamed mixture, mixing well (mixture will be stiff).

Divide dough into fourths. Mix small amount yellow food coloring and lemon rind into one part. Mix small amount orange food coloring and orange rind into second part. Mix small amount green food coloring and lime rind into third part. Leave remaining part plain.

Shape each portion of colored dough into a roll, 2 inches in diameter. Divide plain dough into 3 equal portions; roll each portion into a 6-inch square. Wrap square of

dough around each roll of colored dough; press together. Roll each in matching colored sugar. (To make colored sugar, stir a small amount liquid food coloring into granulated sugar, blending until desired color is achieved.) Cover and refrigerate several hours.

Cut rolls into ¼-inch slices; cut each slice in half. Arrange on ungreased cookie sheets. Bake at 400° for 6 to 8 minutes. Remove to wire racks and cool completely.

Pipe Royal Icing on cookies to resemble fruit sections using metal tip No. 3. Let dry thoroughly. Yield: 6 to 7 dozen.

Royal Icing:
1 large egg white
⅛ teaspoon cream of tartar
1¾ cups sifted powdered sugar

Combine egg white and cream of tartar in a large mixing bowl. Beat at medium speed of an electric mixer until frothy. Gradually add powdered sugar, mixing well. Beat for 5 minutes. Yield: about ⅔ cup.

Note: Royal Icing dries very quickly; keep covered at all times with plastic wrap.

JAVA GEMS
3 cups sugar
Dash of salt
½ cup half-and-half
2 tablespoons instant coffee powder
2 tablespoons light corn syrup
1 cup milk
3 tablespoons butter or margarine
1 teaspoon vanilla extract
Diced candied red pineapple (optional)

Combine first 6 ingredients in a heavy 3-quart saucepan; cook over low heat, stirring constantly, until sugar dissolves. Continue cooking, without stirring, until mixture reaches soft-ball stage (234°). Remove from heat, and add butter and vanilla (do not stir). Cool mixture to lukewarm (110°).

Beat at medium speed of electric mixer until mixture begins to thicken. Pour into a buttered 8-inch square pan. Cool completely. Cut into 1-inch diamonds. Garnish with candied pineapple. Yield: about 5 dozen.

GLAZED SPICE BARS
¾ cup vegetable oil
¼ cup honey
1 cup sugar
1 egg
2 cups all-purpose flour
1 teaspoon baking soda
½ teaspoon salt
1 teaspoon ground cinnamon
1 cup chopped walnuts
Glaze (recipe follows)

Combine first 9 ingredients and mix well. (Dough will be stiff.) Pack into an ungreased 13- x 9- x 2-inch baking pan. Bake at 350° for 25 to 30 minutes. Let cool; then drizzle glaze over top. Cut into bars. Yield: about 3 dozen.

Glaze:
½ cup sifted powdered sugar
½ teaspoon vanilla extract
1 teaspoon water
1½ teaspoons mayonnaise

Combine all ingredients, mixing until smooth. Yield: about ¼ cup.

CREME DE CACAO BALLS
2½ cups crushed chocolate sandwich
  cookies
1 cup chopped walnuts
1 cup sifted powdered sugar
⅓ cup créme de cacao
2 tablespoons dark corn syrup
Powdered sugar

Combine crushed cookies, walnuts, and 1 cup powdered sugar in a large bowl. Add créme de cacao and corn syrup, mixing thoroughly. Shape mixture into 1-inch balls, and roll each in powdered sugar. Place in an airtight container and chill overnight. Yield: 3 dozen.

ALMOND FUDGE RING
1 cup whole almonds
1 (6-ounce) package semisweet chocolate
  morsels
1 (6-ounce) package butterscotch morsels
1 (14-ounce) can sweetened condensed
  milk
1 cup coarsely chopped almonds
½ teaspoon vanilla extract
Red and green candied cherries
Sliced almonds

Line bottom of a 9-inch piepan with a 12-inch square of aluminum foil. Place a custard cup in center of pan. Place whole almonds around custard cup, forming a 2-inch-wide ring; set aside.
Combine chocolate and butterscotch morsels and sweetened condensed milk in the top of a double boiler; place over hot (not boiling) water. Stir until morsels have melted and mixture begins to thicken. Remove mixture from heat; stir in chopped almonds and vanilla. Chill about 1 hour.
Spoon chocolate-butterscotch mixture in mounds over whole almonds; remove custard cup. Decorate with candied cherries and sliced almonds. Yield: one 8-inch ring.

Have an assortment of Christmas goodies on hand throughout the season. Youngsters of all ages will enjoy these Slice of Fruit Cookies!

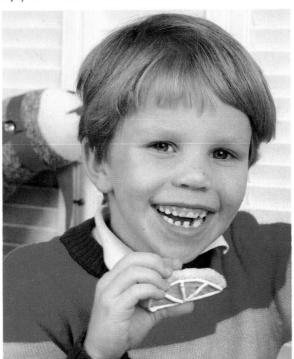

YULE LOG

¾ cup sifted cake flour
¼ cup cocoa
¼ teaspoon salt
5 eggs, separated
1 cup sugar
1 tablespoon lemon juice
2 to 3 tablespoons powdered sugar
Cream Filling
Mocha Frosting
Whipped cream
Crushed peppermint

Grease both the bottom and sides of a 15- x 10- x 1-inch jellyroll pan with vegetable oil; line with waxed paper, and grease lightly. Set aside.

Sift together flour, cocoa, and salt; beat egg yolks at high speed of an electric mixer 5 minutes or until thick. Gradually add sugar, beating well. Stir in lemon juice, and set mixture aside.

Beat egg whites (at room temperature) until stiff but not dry. Gently fold yolk mixture into whites. Gradually fold flour mixture into egg mixture. Spread batter evenly in prepared pan. Bake at 350° for 15 minutes.

Sift powdered sugar in a 15- x 10-inch rectangle on a linen towel. When cake is done, loosen from sides of pan immediately, and turn out onto sugar. Peel off waxed paper. Starting at narrow end, roll up cake and towel together; cool cake on a wire rack, seam side down.

Unroll cake; remove towel. Spread cake with Cream Filling, and reroll. Place on serving plate, seam side down; chill at least 1 hour.

Spread Mocha Frosting over cake roll; chill 1 hour. Garnish with whipped cream and crushed peppermint just before serving. Yield: 10 to 12 servings.

Cream Filling:

¾ cup whipping cream
¼ cup sifted powdered sugar
3 tablespoons finely diced candied red and green cherries

Beat whipping cream until foamy; gradually add powdered sugar, beating until soft peaks form. Stir in candied cherries. Yield: 1½ cups.

Mocha Frosting:

¼ cup strong coffee
6 (1-ounce) squares semisweet chocolate
½ cup butter, cut into small pieces
¼ cup powdered sugar

Heat coffee in a medium saucepan. Add chocolate and butter; cook over low heat, stirring constantly, until creamy and smooth. Remove from heat; stir in powdered sugar. Refrigerate until frosting begins to set. Yield: about 1 cup.

AMBROSIA PIE

2½ tablespoons cornstarch
¾ cup sugar
Pinch of salt
¼ cup cold water
¾ cup boiling water
1 teaspoon grated orange rind
Juice and pulp of 1 large orange
3 eggs, separated
1 teaspoon lemon juice
½ cup flaked coconut
1 baked 9-inch pastry shell
¼ teaspoon plus ⅛ teaspoon cream of
  tartar
¼ cup plus 2 tablespoons sugar

Combine cornstarch, ¾ cup sugar, and salt; add ¼ cup cold water, stirring until smooth. Add boiling water, mixing well. Stir in orange rind, juice, and pulp. Beat egg yolks, and add to orange mixture. Cook over medium heat, stirring constantly, until smooth and thickened. Remove from heat; stir in lemon juice and coconut. Pour into pastry shell.

Beat egg whites (at room temperature) and cream of tartar until foamy. Gradually add sugar, 1 tablespoon at a time, beating until stiff peaks form and sugar dissolves. Spread meringue over filling, sealing to edge of pastry. Bake at 350° for 12 to 15 minutes or until golden brown. Yield: one 9-inch pie.

SPECIAL CARROT CAKE

2 cups all-purpose flour
2 teaspoons baking soda
½ teaspoon salt
2 teaspoons ground cinnamon
3 eggs, well beaten
¾ cup vegetable oil
¾ cup buttermilk
2 cups sugar
2 teaspoons vanilla extract
1 (8-ounce) can crushed pineapple,
  drained
2 cups grated carrot
1 (3½-ounce) can flaked coconut
1 cup chopped walnuts
Cream Cheese Frosting

Combine flour, soda, salt, and cinnamon; set aside. Combine eggs, oil, buttermilk, sugar, and vanilla; beat until smooth. Stir in flour mixture, pineapple, carrot, coconut, and chopped walnuts. Pour batter into 2 greased and floured 9-inch round cakepans.

Bake at 350° for 35 to 40 minutes or until a wooden pick inserted in center comes out clean. Cool in pans 10 minutes; remove from pans, and let cool completely.

Spread Cream Cheese Frosting between layers and on top and sides of cake, spreading frosting smoothly on top, and in swirls on sides. Reserve ½ cup frosting for rosettes. Score top of cake to mark 12 slices. Pipe a rosette on top of each slice using reserved frosting and metal decorating tip No. 20. Store cake in refrigerator. Yield: one 2-layer cake.

Cream Cheese Frosting:

¾ cup butter, softened
4 (3-ounce) packages cream cheese,
  softened
2 teaspoons vanilla extract
3 cups sifted powdered sugar

Combine butter and cream cheese, beating until light and fluffy. Add vanilla and powdered sugar; beat until smooth. Yield: frosting for one 2-layer cake.

APPLE-MINCE PIE

6 cups peeled, minced apple
2 cups raisins
¾ cup firmly packed brown sugar
2 tablespoons all-purpose flour
1½ teaspoons ground cinnamon
1½ teaspoons ground nutmeg
½ teaspoon ground cloves
½ teaspoon salt
1½ cups apple cider or apple juice
1 recipe Double-Crust Pastry

Combine first 9 ingredients in a Dutch oven; cook, uncovered, over low heat 30 minutes, stirring occasionally.

Roll half of pastry onto a lightly floured surface to ⅛-inch thickness; fit into a 9-inch pieplate. Trim pastry overhang to ½-inch from edge of pieplate.

Pour apple mixture into unbaked pie shell. Roll remaining pastry out to ¼-inch thickness on a lightly floured surface; cut into ½-inch strips. Arrange lattice-fashion over apple mixture. Trim strips even with edge of pieplate. Fold bottom pastry over lattice strips; seal and flute. Bake at 375° for 45 minutes. Yield: one 9-inch pie.

Double-Crust Pastry:

2 cups all-purpose flour
1 teaspoon salt
⅔ cup plus 1 tablespoon shortening
4 to 5 tablespoons cold water

Combine flour and salt in a bowl; cut in shortening with pastry blender until mixture resembles coarse meal. Sprinkle cold water, 1 tablespoon at a time, evenly over surface; stir with a fork until dry ingredients are moistened. Shape into a ball; chill. Yield: pastry for one double-crust pie.

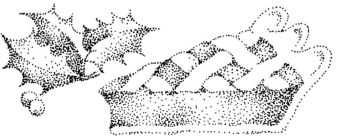

NEIGHBORHOOD POTLUCK SUPPER

Why wait to have a party until you have plenty of time to cook? Just decorate the house, telephone your neighbors, and invite them to a Potluck Supper! This is an old-fashioned way of entertaining whose time has come again. Today's busy schedules allow so little time for elaborate preparations that a spontaneous party, to which each guest brings one dish, is often the best solution.

The test of a good potluck meal is that all of the dishes carry well and require a minimum of last-minute preparation. Each recipe given here is prepared completely ahead of time. Some, like the Layered Vegetable Salad, are served cold and need only a toss before serving. Others, such as the savory Spinach Lasagna, are assembled beforehand and then baked in the oven.

A complete menu is given, in case you and your friends are planning the party together. There is Hearty Beef 'N Beans Casserole, sesame-coated Chicken Nuggets with Sweet-Sour Sauce, vegetables, salads, and a scrumptious Rich Chocolate Cake for serious chocolate-lovers.

HEARTY BEEF 'N BEANS

6 slices bacon
2 medium onions, chopped
1 medium-size green pepper, chopped
1 pound ground beef
2 (16-ounce) cans pork and beans
¾ cup catsup
½ cup firmly packed brown sugar
½ cup molasses
1 teaspoon liquid smoke
¼ teaspoon hot sauce

Cook bacon in a large skillet until almost crisp; remove bacon, reserving 2 tablespoons drippings in skillet. Crumble bacon; set aside.

Add onion, green pepper, and ground beef to drippings. Cook over medium heat until meat is browned, stirring to crumble. Drain off pan drippings.

Combine bacon, meat mixture, and all remaining ingredients; mix well. Spoon mixture into a lightly greased 13- x 9- x 2-inch baking dish. Bake, uncovered, at 425° for 30 minutes or until mixture is bubbly. Yield: 8 to 10 servings.

GARLIC FRENCH BREAD

½ cup butter or margarine, softened
1 clove garlic, minced
⅛ teaspoon dried whole dillweed
1 (16-ounce) loaf French bread

Combine butter, garlic, and dillweed; mix well. Slice bread crosswise into 1-inch slices, cutting to but not through bottom crust. Spread butter mixture between slices of bread. Wrap bread tightly in aluminum foil. Bake at 350° for 15 minutes or until thoroughly heated. Yield: about 10 servings.

ASPARAGUS-PEA CASSEROLE

1 (14½-ounce) can asparagus spears
1 (17-ounce) can green peas
2 hard-cooked eggs, peeled and sliced
Cheese sauce (recipe follows)
¼ cup buttered breadcrumbs
Cherry tomatoes (optional)

Drain asparagus spears and peas, reserving liquid. Cut asparagus into 1-inch pieces. Set aside a few asparagus tips to use for garnish. Arrange half of vegetables in a 1½-quart casserole; place two sliced eggs on top. Pour half of cheese sauce over eggs. Repeat layers. Sprinkle breadcrumbs on top. Bake at 350° for 20 minutes or until thoroughly heated. Garnish with asparagus tips and cherry tomatoes. Yield: 8 servings.

Cheese Sauce:
3 tablespoons butter or margarine
3½ tablespoons all-purpose flour
½ cup reserved liquid from asparagus and peas
½ pound process American cheese, cut into 1-inch cubes

Melt butter in a heavy saucepan over low heat; add flour and cook 1 minute, stirring constantly. Gradually add ½ cup reserved liquid from asparagus and peas. Cook over medium heat, stirring constantly, until thickened. Add cheese and stir until smooth. Yield: about 1 cup.

NO-COOK APRICOT CANDIES

3 (6-ounce) packages dried apricots, cut into small pieces
1 (14-ounce) package flaked coconut
1 cup chopped walnuts
1 (14-ounce) can sweetened condensed milk
½ cup powdered sugar

Combine apricots, coconut, and walnuts in a large bowl; add condensed milk, mixing well. Shape into 1-inch balls, and roll each in powdered sugar. Yield: about 9 dozen.

FRUIT SALAD WITH POPPY SEED DRESSING

2 large green apples, unpeeled, cored, and cut into wedges
2 large red apples, unpeeled, cored, and cut into wedges
3 tablespoons lemon juice
3 large oranges, peeled and sliced crosswise
¾ cup fresh cranberries
4 kiwi, peeled and sliced crosswise
1 bunch Romaine lettuce, shredded
Poppy Seed Dressing

Toss apple wedges in lemon juice; arrange apples, oranges, cranberries, and kiwi on a bed of lettuce. Drizzle Poppy Seed Dressing over fruit. Yield: 8 to 10 servings.

Poppy Seed Dressing:

½ cup vegetable oil
¼ cup honey
3 tablespoons red wine vinegar
1 tablespoon poppy seeds
2 teaspoons minced onion
1½ teaspoons Dijon mustard
½ teaspoon salt

Combine all ingredients in container of electric blender; process on low speed 30 seconds. Chill thoroughly; stir well before using. Yield: 1 cup.

CHICKEN NUGGETS WITH SWEET-SOUR SAUCE

3 whole chicken breasts, skinned and boned
½ cup all-purpose flour
¾ teaspoon salt
2 teaspoons sesame seeds
1 egg, slightly beaten
½ cup water
Hot vegetable oil
Fresh parsley sprigs (optional)
Sweet-Sour Sauce (recipe follows)

Cut chicken into 1½- x 1-inch pieces; set aside. Combine next 5 ingredients. Dip the chicken into batter; then fry in hot oil (375°) until golden brown. Drain on paper towels. Arrange in serving container and garnish with parsley, if desired. Serve with Sweet-Sour Sauce. Yield: 6 to 8 servings.

Sweet-Sour Sauce:

½ cup firmly packed brown sugar
2 tablespoons cornstarch
¼ cup vinegar
3 tablespoons soy sauce
½ cup pineapple juice
Salt to taste (optional)
Shredded lettuce (optional)

Combine sugar and cornstarch in a small saucepan, stirring well. Gradually add vinegar, soy sauce, and pineapple juice; cook over low heat, stirring constantly, until thick and smooth. Add salt, if desired. Float a few shredded pieces of lettuce on top of sauce, if desired. Yield: about 1 cup.

SPINACH LASAGNA

1 pound ground beef
2 (15½-ounce) jars spaghetti sauce
1 (16-ounce) carton ricotta or small-curd cottage cheese
1½ cups (6 ounces) shredded mozzarella cheese, divided
1 egg
1 (10-ounce) package frozen chopped spinach, thawed and drained
1 teaspoon salt
⅛ teaspoon pepper
¾ teaspoon dried whole oregano
1 (8-ounce) package lasagna noodles, uncooked
1 cup water

Cook ground beef in a large skillet until browned, stirring to crumble meat. Drain off drippings. Stir in spaghetti sauce; set aside.
Combine ricotta cheese, 1 cup mozzarella cheese, egg, spinach, salt, pepper, and oregano in a large bowl; stir well. Set aside.
Spread ½ cup meat sauce in a greased 13- x 9- x 2-inch baking dish. Place one-third of

the uncooked lasagna noodles over sauce; spread with half of the cheese mixture. Top with one-third of the meat sauce. Repeat layers. Top with remaining noodles, meat sauce, and ½ cup reserved mozzarella cheese; pour water around edges.

Cover securely with aluminum foil, and bake at 350° for 1 hour and 15 minutes. Let stand 15 minutes before serving. Yield: 8 servings.

LAYERED VEGETABLE SALAD
4 cups torn fresh mixed salad greens
2 cups diced raw cauliflower
½ cup chopped celery
¼ cup chopped onion
3 hard-cooked eggs, chopped
¼ cup chopped sweet pickle
½ cup commercial sour cream
½ cup mayonnaise
½ cup (2 ounces) shredded Cheddar cheese
½ cup diced green pepper
6 slices bacon, cooked and crumbled

Place greens in a large bowl. Layer cauliflower, celery, onion, eggs, and sweet pickle on top of greens.

Combine sour cream and mayonnaise. Spread over vegetable mixture, sealing to edge of bowl. Sprinkle with shredded cheese and green pepper. Cover and chill overnight.

Sprinkle with bacon, and toss salad just before serving. Yield: 8 to 10 servings.

EASY BEAN SALAD
1 (16-ounce) can green beans, drained
1 (16-ounce) can wax beans, drained
1 (15-ounce) can kidney beans, rinsed and drained
1 (2-ounce) jar diced pimiento, drained
1 medium-size green pepper, sliced
1 medium onion, sliced
½ cup vegetable oil
½ cup cider vinegar
¾ cup sugar
1½ teaspoons salt
½ teaspoon pepper

Combine vegetables, stirring gently. Combine remaining ingredients; pour over vegetables, stirring gently to blend. Cover and chill overnight. Yield: 8 servings.

RICH CHOCOLATE CAKE
½ cup butter, softened
1 (16-ounce) package brown sugar
3 eggs
3 (1-ounce) squares unsweetened chocolate, melted
2¼ cups sifted cake flour
2 teaspoons baking soda
½ teaspoon salt
1 cup commercial sour cream
1 cup hot water
1½ teaspoons vanilla extract
Frosting (recipe follows)
½ cup chopped walnuts

Cream butter; gradually add sugar, beating well. Add eggs, one at a time, beating after each addition. Add chocolate, mixing well.

Combine flour, soda, and salt; gradually add to chocolate mixture alternately with sour cream, beating well after each addition. Add water, mixing well; stir in vanilla. (The batter will be thin.)

Pour batter into a greased and floured 13- x 9- x 2-inch baking pan. Bake at 350° for 40 minutes or until wooden pick inserted in center comes out clean; cool. Spread frosting on cake; sprinkle with walnuts. Yield: 15 servings.

Frosting:
½ cup semisweet chocolate morsels
¼ cup half-and-half
¼ cup plus 2 tablespoons butter or margarine
1¼ cups sifted powdered sugar

Combine chocolate morsels, half-and-half, and butter in a saucepan; cook over medium heat, stirring until chocolate melts. Remove from heat; add powdered sugar, mixing well.

Set saucepan in ice, and beat until frosting holds its shape and loses its gloss. Yield: about 1½ cups.

GIFTS FROM YOUR KITCHEN

> CURRIED SUNFLOWER SEEDS
> LEMON-CRANBERRY SAUCE
> MUNCHIES
> BOUQUET GARNI
> MIXED FRUIT CHUTNEY
> BAKLAVA
> QUICK MIX
> ALMOND BUTTER
> GERMAN CHRISTMAS COOKIES

Think of Christmas, and you'll probably think of food next. Because almost everyone loves to receive food as a gift, you can spend a while in the kitchen and save yourself hours of shopping. Furthermore, the gift always fits!

Some of the gifts are made well ahead, while others are made closer to the day you'll need them. All of them may be made even more appealing by the way in which they are packaged. Use your imagination in coming up with containers—a bow, a doily, or a hand-painted plastic box can add immensely to the appearance of your food, and the lucky recipient will appreciate your thoughtfulness long after the last crumb has been eaten.

CURRIED SUNFLOWER SEEDS
3 cups raw sunflower kernels
1 tablespoon butter, melted
2 teaspoons seasoned salt
¾ teaspoon curry powder

Place sunflower kernels in a shallow roasting pan; drizzle butter over kernels, and stir well. Bake at 350° for 20 minutes or until golden brown, stirring once.

Combine salt and curry powder; sprinkle over sunflower kernels, and stir until coated. Return to oven and bake an additional 10 minutes. Drain on paper towels; cool. Store in an airtight container. Yield: 3 cups.

LEMON-CRANBERRY SAUCE
4 cups fresh cranberries
2 oranges
2 cups sugar
1 (3-ounce) package lemon-flavored gelatin
1½ cups boiling water
½ cup chopped celery
½ cup chopped walnuts

Carefully sort and wash cranberries; drain. Quarter and seed oranges. Coarsely grind cranberries and oranges in a food grinder or blender. Combine cranberry mixture and sugar; stir well and let stand until sugar dissolves.

Dissolve gelatin in boiling water; cool. Add gelatin, celery, and walnuts to cranberry mixture; stir well. Pack in gift jars and chill until ready to serve. This is a delicious accompaniment to poultry. Yield: 2 quarts.

MUNCHIES
1 (5-ounce) can chow mein noodles
1 cup whole almonds
1½ cups round oat cereal
1½ cups miniature shredded wheat or rice cereal squares
⅓ cup butter or margarine, melted
1 tablespoon Worcestershire sauce
½ teaspoon chili powder
½ teaspoon celery salt
⅛ teaspoon garlic powder

In a large bowl, combine first 4 ingredients. Combine remaining ingredients, and pour over cereal mixture. Stir until evenly distributed. Spread coated cereal mixture on an ungreased 15- x 10- x 1-inch jellyroll pan. Bake at 300° for 15 to 20 minutes, stirring once. Yield: 7 cups.

Give your friends a gift from your own kitchen. Clockwise from front: German Christmas Cookies, Bouquets Garnis, Lemon-Cranberry Sauce, Curried Sunflower Seeds, Munchies, Quick Mix in cloth bags (instructions for making bags on page 77), Almond Butter.

Lemon-Cranberry Sauce and Bouquets Garnis are ideal for holiday giving.

BOUQUET GARNI
1 tablespoon dried parsley flakes
1 teaspoon dried whole thyme
¼ teaspoon dried whole rosemary
4 whole peppercorns
1 bay leaf

Place all ingredients together in a square made of cheesecloth; wrap tightly with cotton twine to hold. Store in an airtight container. Use for seasoning soups, stocks, and sauces. Yield: one bouquet garni.

MIXED FRUIT CHUTNEY
1 cup fresh orange sections
¼ cup orange juice
4 cups cranberries
2 cups sugar
1 cup chopped, unpeeled apple
½ cup raisins
¼ cup chopped walnuts
1 tablespoon vinegar
½ teaspoon ground ginger
½ teaspoon ground cinnamon

Combine all ingredients in a large saucepan and bring to a boil. Reduce heat and simmer 5 minutes or until berries begin to burst. Chill until serving time. Serve with pork, ham, or poultry. Yield: 5½ cups.

BAKLAVA
1 pound frozen fillo pastry
1 cup butter, melted
1 cup ground walnuts
⅓ cup ground almonds
2 tablespoons sugar
½ teaspoon ground cinnamon
½ teaspoon ground nutmeg
Syrup (recipe follows)

Thaw fillo. Cut fillo in half crosswise; then cut each half to fit a 13- x 9- x 2-inch baking pan. Cover with a slightly damp towel.

Lightly butter the bottom of pan. Layer 10 sheets of fillo in pan, brushing each sheet with melted butter.

Combine walnuts, almonds, sugar, and spices, mixing well. Sprinkle half the nut mixture over fillo in pan; drizzle with a little melted butter. Top nut mixture with 20 additional sheets of fillo, brushing each with butter; top with remaining nut mixture. Drizzle a little melted butter over nut mixture. Top with remaining fillo, brushing each sheet with melted butter. Cut fillo into diamond shapes. Bake at 350° for 50 minutes. Cool thoroughly. Drizzle warm syrup over pastries. Let stand at room temperature 24 hours. Yield: about 3½ dozen.

Syrup:
½ cup sugar
¼ cup water
1 tablespoon lemon juice
2½ tablespoons honey

Combine sugar, water, and lemon juice; bring to a boil and boil 7 minutes. Add honey and boil 3 additional minutes. Yield: ½ cup.

QUICK MIX

12 cups all-purpose flour
2 tablespoons salt
¼ cup plus 2 tablespoons baking powder
2 cups shortening

Combine first 3 ingredients. Cut in shortening with pastry blender until mixture resembles coarse meal. Place in covered container. Store in refrigerator or a cool place. Yield: about 14 cups.

Muffins:

2 cups Quick Mix
2 tablespoons sugar
1 egg, beaten
¾ cup milk

Combine first 2 ingredients; make a well in center of mixture. Combine egg and milk; add to dry ingredients, stirring just until moistened. Spoon into greased muffin pans, filling two-thirds full. Bake at 425° for 15 to 20 minutes. Yield: 10 muffins.

Pancakes:

2 cups Quick Mix
1¼ cups milk
2 eggs, beaten

Combine all ingredients, stirring well. Drop mixture by ¼ cupfuls onto a hot, lightly greased griddle. Turn pancakes when tops are covered with bubbles and edges are brown. Serve hot with syrup. Yield: about 1 dozen pancakes.

ALMOND BUTTER

1 cup butter or margarine, softened
¼ teaspoon almond extract
¼ cup finely chopped almonds

Beat butter until smooth and creamy. Add almond extract and almonds, stirring well. Pack firmly into small ramekins and chill. Yield: 1¼ cups.

GERMAN CHRISTMAS COOKIES

1 cup honey
¾ cup firmly packed brown sugar
1 egg, beaten
1 tablespoon lemon juice
2¼ cups all-purpose flour
¾ teaspoon ground cinnamon
½ teaspoon ground allspice
½ teaspoon ground nutmeg
¼ teaspoon ground cloves
½ teaspoon salt
½ teaspoon baking soda
¼ cup finely chopped almonds
⅓ cup finely chopped candied citron
Candied red cherry halves
Whole blanched almonds
1 cup plus 2 tablespoons sifted powdered
   sugar
¼ cup plus 1 tablespoon rum or water

Heat honey in a medium saucepan just until warm. Stir in next 3 ingredients and set aside.

Combine dry ingredients in a large bowl. Add honey mixture, almonds, and citron; stir until blended. Cover and chill overnight.

Work with one-fourth of dough at a time, keeping remaining dough chilled. Roll dough to ⅜-inch thickness on a heavily-floured surface. Cut dough into 2½-inch rounds and transfer to greased cookie sheets. Press a candied cherry half in center of each, and arrange 5 whole almonds radiating from center of each cherry. Bake at 375° for 12 minutes or until golden brown. Transfer to racks.

Combine powdered sugar and rum; stir until blended. Immediately brush rum mixture over hot cookies. Let cool completely. Store in airtight container. Yield: about 2 dozen.

Note: When first baked, cookies are hard and crunchy. They are typically stored in an airtight container for 2 weeks to soften, although they may be eaten earlier, if desired.

OLD WORLD BREADS

SWEDISH LUCIA BUNS
MEXICAN THREE KINGS BREAD
ITALIAN PANETTONE
SCANDINAVIAN CHRISTMAS BRAID
DUTCH OLIEBOLLEN

Nothing says "Home" quite so much as the smell of freshly baked bread. Its yeasty aroma, drifting from behind the kitchen door, beckons child and grownup alike to come and see when it will be ready. Of all foods, bread is the most nearly universal.

Cooks throughout the world have created breads to reflect their customs. Every land has breads, unique in shape or flavor, which over the years have become traditional to serve at holidays. Many Americans whose forebears came from other countries within recent memory still bake these breads every Christmas to symbolize the rich heritage of their families. Often the bread has a symbolic meaning, and children are told of Old World customs each time it is served, giving them a sense of being part of something large and wonderful.

Italians have their Panettone, filled with plump raisins and candied fruits. The Scandinavians have their lovely braided bread, flavored with cardamom and sprinkled with almonds. The Dutch enjoy their fried Oliebollen dusted with cinnamon, the Mexicans their wreath-shaped Three Kings Bread, and the Swedes their Lucia Buns that honor Saint Lucia and usher in the Christmas Season.

Enjoy the flavors of some of the world's best breads this year by sampling the recipes given here. Bring out the box of old, faded photographs, tell the story of your family's arrival in this country, and serve some bread. You may even start a new tradition in your own family.

SWEDISH LUCIA BUNS

½ cup water
½ cup milk
¼ cup plus 2 tablespoons butter or
    margarine
1 package dry yeast
½ cup sugar
1 egg, beaten
½ teaspoon salt
⅛ teaspoon ground saffron
3½ to 4 cups all-purpose flour, divided
Raisins
1 egg white
1 tablespoon water

Heat water, milk, and butter in a Dutch oven until butter melts. Remove from heat and cool to lukewarm (105° to 115°). Dissolve the yeast in milk mixture; let stand 5 minutes. Stir in sugar, egg, salt, saffron, and 2 cups flour; mix well. Gradually stir in enough remaining flour to make a soft dough.

Turn dough out onto a floured surface and knead until smooth and elastic (about 8 to 10 minutes). Place in a well-greased bowl, turning to grease top. Cover and let rise in a warm place (85°), free from drafts, 1 hour or until doubled in bulk.

Punch dough down; turn out onto lightly floured surface, and knead 1 minute. Divide into 24 equal parts; roll each part into a 12-inch rope. Form 2 ropes into "S" shapes, coiling ends of each rope in opposite directions. Lay one "S" rope perpendicularly across another "S" rope on greased baking sheet. Insert a raisin in center of each coil. Repeat with remaining ropes. Cover and let rise in a warm place, free from drafts, 30 minutes or until almost doubled in bulk.

Combine egg white and water; brush over buns. Bake at 350° for 17 minutes or until golden brown. Cool on wire racks. Yield: 1 dozen.

Celebrate Christmas with breads from other countries. Clockwise from front: Italian Panettone, Dutch Oliebollen, Scandinavian Christmas Braid, Mexican Three Kings Bread, Swedish Lucia Buns.

MEXICAN THREE KINGS BREAD

½ cup water
¼ cup sugar
½ teaspoon salt
¼ cup butter or margarine
1 package dry yeast
3 tablespoons warm milk (105° to 115°)
1 egg
3 cups all-purpose flour, divided
½ cup chopped walnuts
½ cup chopped red and green candied
  cherries
1½ cups sifted powdered sugar
2 to 3 tablespoons water
Candied pineapple rings
Candied red and green cherries

Combine ½ cup water, sugar, salt, and butter in a small saucepan. Cook over low heat until butter melts; cool to lukewarm (110°).

Dissolve yeast in warm milk in a large bowl; let stand 5 minutes. Stir in lukewarm butter mixture. Add egg and 2 cups flour; beat at medium speed of an electric mixer until blended. Stir in enough remaining flour to make a soft dough.

Turn dough out onto a lightly floured surface, and knead until smooth and elastic (about 8 to 10 minutes). Shape into a ball and place in a well-greased bowl, turning to grease top. Cover and let rise in a warm place (85°), free from drafts, 1 hour or until doubled in bulk.

Punch dough down, and knead in walnuts and chopped cherries until evenly distributed. Shape dough into a 24-inch rope. Place rope in a greased 6½ cup ring mold with smooth sides. Pinch ends together to seal. Cover and let rise in a warm place (85°), free from drafts, 45 minutes or until doubled in bulk. Bake at 375° for 20 to 25 minutes or until golden brown. Remove from pan and let cool on wire rack.

Combine powdered sugar and enough water to make mixture a smooth spreading consistency. Spread evenly over bread, smoothing with the back of a spoon. Decorate with candied fruit. Yield: one loaf.

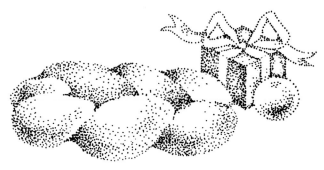

ITALIAN PANETTONE

2 packages dry yeast
1 cup warm milk (105° to 115°)
½ cup sugar
½ cup butter or margarine, softened
3 eggs, beaten
1 teaspoon salt
5 to 5½ cups all-purpose flour, divided
⅔ cup raisins
½ cup chopped mixed candied fruit
1 egg white
1 teaspoon water
½ to 1 tablespoon sugar

Dissolve yeast in warm milk in a large bowl; let stand 5 minutes. Add ½ cup sugar, butter, eggs, salt, and 3 cups flour. Beat at medium speed of electric mixer until smooth. Stir in enough remaining flour to make a soft dough.

Turn dough out onto a lightly floured surface and knead until smooth and elastic (about 5 minutes). Place dough in a greased bowl, turning to grease top. Cover and let rise in a warm place (85°), free from drafts, 1½ hours or until doubled in bulk.

Grease the bottom and sides of an 8-inch springform pan; set aside. Punch the dough down. Knead in raisins and fruit until evenly distributed. Place dough in prepared pan. Cover and let rise in a warm place (85°), free from drafts, 1 hour or until doubled in bulk. Cut a cross in center of loaf with a knife. Combine egg white and water; brush over loaf.

Bake at 350° for 30 minutes. Remove loaf from oven. Brush with additional egg white mixture, and sprinkle with ½ to 1 tablespoon sugar. Cover loosely with foil; bake an additional 30 minutes or until bread sounds hollow when tapped. Remove from pan; cool on wire rack. Yield: 1 loaf.

SCANDINAVIAN CHRISTMAS BRAID

2 packages dry yeast
¾ cup warm water (105° to 115°)
½ cup sugar
½ teaspoon salt
½ cup butter or margarine, softened
2 eggs
3½ to 4 cups all-purpose flour, divided
1 teaspoon ground cardamom
¾ cup coarsely chopped red and green
    candied cherries
¾ cup raisins
1 egg white
1 teaspoon water
2 teaspoons sugar
2 tablespoons chopped almonds

Dissolve yeast in warm water in a large mixing bowl; let stand 5 minutes. Stir in sugar and salt.

Add butter, eggs, 2½ cups flour, and cardamom; beat at medium speed of an electric mixer 2 minutes or until smooth.

Gradually stir in enough remaining flour to make a soft dough. Turn dough out onto a floured surface, and knead until smooth and elastic (about 5 minutes). Place in a well-greased bowl, turning to grease top. Cover and let rise in a warm place (85°), free from drafts, 1 hour or until doubled in bulk. Punch dough down; add cherries and raisins, and knead until evenly distributed. Divide dough into 6 equal portions. Roll each portion into an 18-inch rope. Braid 3 ropes together, pinching at ends to join ropes. Place braid on a large greased baking sheet. Braid remaining 3 ropes together, and place on top of first braid. Cover and let rise in a warm place (85°), free from drafts, 1 hour or until doubled in bulk.

Combine egg white and water; brush over braid. Sprinkle with sugar and almonds; bake at 375° for 20 minutes. Cover with aluminum foil; bake an additional 10 minutes or until braid sounds hollow when tapped. Cool on wire rack. Yield: 1 loaf.

DUTCH OLIEBOLLEN

2 cups all-purpose flour, divided
1 package dry yeast
½ cup milk
2 tablespoons shortening
2 tablespoons sugar
¼ teaspoon salt
½ teaspoon vanilla extract
2 eggs
¼ cup raisins
¼ cup chopped candied cherries
Vegetable oil
3 tablespoons sugar
½ teaspoon ground cinnamon

Combine 1 cup flour and yeast in a large mixing bowl and set aside. Combine milk, shortening, 2 tablespoons sugar, and salt in a small saucepan. Cook over low heat just until warm (115° to 120°), stirring until shortening melts. Stir in vanilla.

Add milk mixture to flour mixture, stirring well. Add eggs, beating at low speed of an electric mixer until blended. Beat at high speed 2 minutes.

Stir in raisins, candied cherries, and remaining flour. Cover and let rise in a warm place (85°), free from drafts, 30 minutes or until doubled in bulk.

Drop dough by tablespoonfuls into hot oil (375°). Fry about 3 minutes, turning to brown all sides. Drain on paper towels.

Combine sugar and cinnamon; roll each in sugar mixture while still warm. Yield: 1½ dozen.

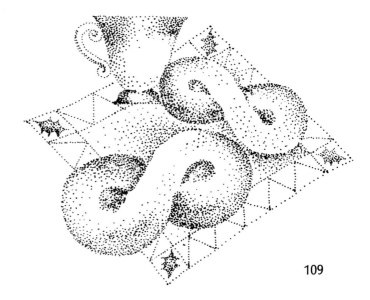

MICROWAVE HELPS

HOT CHILE-CHEESE DIP
CRABMEAT CANAPÉS
FLOUNDER AMANDINE
GLAZED HAM LOAF
TURKEY A LA KING
PARTY MEATBALLS
MICROWAVE BANANAS FOSTER
CHOCOLATE ESPRESSO

Holidays are busy days—when cooking sometimes takes second place to shopping, wrapping, parties, and friends. This is the perfect time to let your microwave oven help you. One of these recipes for hors d'oeuvres, main dishes, desserts, and a beverage may be just what you need for a quick meal or a treat to serve when your guests arrive unexpectedly.

If you enjoy hot hors d'oeuvres, you'll want to remember these recipes for parties even after the holidays. The Hot Chile-Cheese Dip made from processed cheese is delicious on corn chips or spooned over a baked potato. The Crabmeat Canapés are elegant tidbits to serve with cocktails, and the pungent Party Meatballs are so popular that hungry guests are apt to stand in line.

For a main dish, serve the Flounder Amandine cooked with butter and a generous helping of almonds or the Glazed Ham Loaf with its topping of cranberry sauce. If you are trying to use the last bit of turkey, the Turkey a La King is a good choice.

On occasions that call for a spectacular dessert, you and your guests would enjoy the flaming Microwave Bananas Foster. At the end of an especially busy day, treat yourself by relaxing in front of the fire with a steaming cup of Chocolate Espresso.

If company drops in unexpectedly, you can have Hot Chile-Cheese Dip in a matter of minutes with the aid of a microwave oven. Garnish the dip with shredded lettuce, green onions, and ripe olives, serving chips on the side.

HOT CHILE-CHEESE DIP

1 (16-ounce) package processed cheese
   spread, cut into 1-inch cubes
1 (4-ounce) can chopped green chiles,
   undrained
2 tablespoons milk
⅛ teaspoon garlic powder
Shredded lettuce
Chopped green onions
Sliced ripe olives

Combine first 4 ingredients in a 2-quart microwave-safe baking dish. Cover and microwave at MEDIUM (50% power) for 9 minutes or until cheese melts, stirring every 3 minutes.

Garnish with lettuce, green onions, and olives. Serve with tortilla chips. Yield: 2¼ cups.

CRABMEAT CANAPÉS

2 tablespoons butter or margarine
1 (3-ounce) package cream cheese
⅓ cup canned crabmeat, drained
2 tablespoons mayonnaise
1 egg yolk
1 tablespoon chopped green onion
¼ teaspoon prepared mustard
24 melba toast rounds

Place the butter and cream cheese in a medium-size glass bowl; cover with heavy-duty plastic wrap. Microwave at MEDIUM-HIGH (70% power) for 1 minute or until softened.

Shred crabmeat with a fork. Add crabmeat and remaining ingredients except toast rounds to cream cheese mixture, and mix well. Spread crabmeat mixture evenly on toast rounds.

Arrange 8 toast rounds on a microwave-safe serving dish. Microwave at MEDIUM-HIGH for 30 to 50 seconds or until mixture is set, giving dish a half-turn halfway through cooking. Repeat cooking procedure with remaining canapés. Yield: 2 dozen.

FLOUNDER AMANDINE

¼ cup butter or margarine
¼ cup sliced almonds
1½ teaspoons lemon juice
1 (16-ounce) package frozen flounder (or
    other fish) fillets, thawed
Salt to taste
Paprika
Lemon slices and parsley sprigs

Note: Any frozen fish fillet may be substituted for flounder.

Place butter, almonds, and lemon juice in a 12- x 8- x 2-inch baking dish. Microwave at HIGH for 4 to 6 minutes or until almonds are golden, stirring twice. Remove almonds and set aside, reserving butter mixture in baking dish.

Sprinkle fillets with salt, and coat with butter mixture; sprinkle with paprika. Arrange in dish with thickest portion to outside (thinner portions may overlap, if necessary). Cover with clear plastic wrap.

Microwave at HIGH for 2 to 4 minutes or until fish flakes easily when tested with a fork, giving dish one half-turn during cooking. Carefully remove fish to a serving platter; spoon almonds over top. Garnish with lemon slices and parsley. Yield: 4 servings.

GLAZED HAM LOAF

¾ pound fully cooked ham, ground
¾ pound ground raw pork
1 cup soft breadcrumbs
¼ cup finely chopped onion
2 eggs, beaten
¼ cup chili sauce
1 teaspoon dry mustard
1 cup whole-berry cranberry sauce

Combine first 7 ingredients and mix well. Press mixture into a 9-inch pieplate; cover with waxed paper. Microwave at MEDIUM HIGH (70% power) 12 to 14 minutes or until firm to the touch, giving dish a half-turn after 6 minutes. Drain off drippings.

Spoon cranberry sauce over loaf. Microwave at MEDIUM HIGH for 2 to 4 minutes. Let stand 5 minutes. Yield: 6 servings.

TURKEY A LA KING

2 tablespoons butter or margarine
½ cup chopped green pepper
½ cup sliced fresh mushrooms
1 (10¾-ounce) can cream of celery soup,
    undiluted
2 tablespoons diced pimiento
2 tablespoons water
1 teaspoon sugar
½ teaspoon salt
1 teaspoon Worcestershire sauce
2 cups cubed cooked turkey or chicken
6 frozen patty shells or hot cooked rice

Place butter in a 4-cup glass measure; microwave at HIGH for 45 seconds. Add green pepper and mushrooms; microwave at HIGH 2 minutes, stirring once. Add the soup, pimiento, water, sugar, salt, and Worcestershire sauce; microwave at HIGH 1 to 2 minutes. Stir in turkey; microwave at HIGH 3½ to 4 minutes.

Bake patty shells according to package directions. Serve turkey mixture over patty shells. Yield: 6 servings.

PARTY MEATBALLS

2 pounds bulk pork sausage
2 eggs
1 tablespoon plus 1 teaspoon instant
    minced onions
⅔ cup commercial chili sauce
1 cup commercial grape jelly
2 tablespoons water

Combine first 3 ingredients; mixing thoroughly. Shape sausage mixture into 1½-inch balls. Arrange meatballs in a 12- x 8- x 2-inch baking dish; cover dish loosely with heavy-duty plastic wrap. Microwave at HIGH for 8 to 9 minutes, turning meatballs over, and rearranging them after 4 minutes. Drain off pan drippings.

Combine all remaining ingredients in a microwave-safe dish; stir with a wire whisk until blended. Microwave at HIGH for 2 to 3 minutes. Pour over meatballs. Microwave at HIGH for 2 minutes, stirring once. Yield: 3 dozen.

Serve steaming Chocolate Espresso to guests on a cold night; top with whipped cream and cinnamon.

MICROWAVE BANANAS FOSTER

½ cup butter or margarine
1 cup firmly packed brown sugar
1 tablespoon imitation banana extract
Dash of ground cinnamon
4 medium bananas, sliced
¼ cup rum
Vanilla ice cream

Place butter in a 2-quart shallow casserole. Microwave at HIGH for 1 minute. Stir in sugar, banana extract, and cinnamon. Microwave at HIGH for 40 to 60 seconds; stir well. Gently stir in bananas. Microwave at HIGH for 1½ to 2 minutes; stir.

Place rum in a 1-cup glass measure; microwave at HIGH for 40 to 45 seconds. Quickly pour over bananas, and immediately ignite with match. While still flaming, serve over ice cream. Yield: 6 servings.

CHOCOLATE ESPRESSO

½ cup water
3 tablespoons sugar
Pinch of salt
1 (1-ounce) square unsweetened
    chocolate
2 cups strong coffee or hot espresso
1½ cups milk
Whipped cream
Ground cinnamon

Combine first 4 ingredients in a 2-quart glass bowl. Microwave at HIGH for 1 to 2 minutes or until chocolate melts. Stir in coffee and milk. Microwave at HIGH for 3 to 4 minutes or until hot. Beat until frothy. Microwave 40 to 60 seconds or until hot. Fill cups; top each serving with whipped cream and sprinkle with cinnamon. Yield: 4 cups.

TRIM THE TREE PARTY

```
┌─────────────────────────────────────┐
│        CHEESE TREE    CRACKERS        │
│        CREAMY MUSHROOM SOUP           │
│        HAM-TOPPED POTATOES            │
│        CHILI-TOPPED POTATOES          │
│           VEGETABLE PITAS             │
│    MOCHA MERINGUE-ICE CREAM PIE       │
│     CHRISTMAS FORTUNE COOKIES         │
│           HOT FRUIT PUNCH             │
└─────────────────────────────────────┘
```

There is no better time for a get-together with a few good friends than the evening you spend decorating the tree. Spirits are naturally high with anticipation, and the excitement and laughter of the occasion puts everyone in a party mood.

If you wonder how you could possibly decorate a tree and serve dinner on the same evening, the answer is easy. Let your guests help themselves from food you have prepared ahead of time.

For an unusual end to the meal, serve homemade Christmas Fortune Cookies with a message tucked inside. This is your chance to try your hand at being a writer. Your friends will have many a chuckle when they remember their fortune and the evening you shared.

CREAMY MUSHROOM SOUP

1 large onion, minced
3 tablespoons butter or margarine, melted
1 pound fresh mushrooms, sliced
¼ cup all-purpose flour
6 cups beef consommé
1⅓ cups whipping cream
Pinch of ground nutmeg
Pinch of pepper

Sauté onion in butter in a Dutch oven over medium heat until tender. Add mushrooms; cook over low heat 10 minutes. Stir in flour; cook 4 minutes, stirring constantly. Gradually add consommé; bring to a boil, stirring often. Remove from heat; stir in whipping cream, nutmeg, and pepper. Serve immediately. Yield: 8 servings.

HAM-TOPPED POTATOES

8 large baking potatoes
Vegetable oil
1 chicken-flavored bouillon cube
½ cup hot water
1½ cups milk
¼ cup butter or margarine
¼ cup all-purpose flour
½ cup (2 ounces) shredded process American cheese
1 teaspoon Worcestershire sauce
2 cups cubed cooked ham
⅓ cup sliced, pitted ripe olives
2 tablespoons diced pimiento
2 tablespoons minced fresh parsley

Wash potatoes and rub with oil. Bake at 400° for 1 hour or until soft when pierced with a fork.

Dissolve bouillon cube in hot water; stir in milk, and set aside. Melt butter in a heavy saucepan over low heat; add flour, stirring until smooth. Cook 1 minute, stirring constantly. Gradually add bouillon mixture; cook over medium heat, stirring constantly, until mixture is thickened and bubbly. Add cheese and Worcestershire, stirring until cheese melts. Stir in ham, olives, pimiento, and parsley. Heat thoroughly.

Split tops of potatoes lengthwise, and fluff pulp with a fork. Spoon topping over potatoes. Yield: 8 servings.

HOT FRUIT PUNCH

4 cups cranberry juice cocktail
4 cups unsweetened pineapple juice
2 cups water
½ cup firmly packed brown sugar
2 tablespoons lemon juice
2 (4-inch) sticks cinnamon, broken
2 teaspoons whole cloves
Cinnamon sticks (optional)

Pour first 3 ingredients into a 12-cup percolator. Place remaining ingredients, except whole cinnamon sticks, in percolator basket. Perk through complete cycle of electric percolator. Serve with cinnamon stick stirrers, if desired. Yield: 10 cups.

Invite your friends to help trim the tree and serve this delicious dinner. Clockwise from right: Vegetable Pitas, Ham Topping, Chili Topping, and condiments of green onion, shredded Cheddar cheese, and crumbled bacon to sprinkle over baked potato halves. In background, Hot Fruit Punch with cinnamon stick stirrers.

MOCHA MERINGUE-ICE CREAM PIE

3 egg whites
½ teaspoon baking powder
¾ cup sugar
Pinch of salt
1 cup chocolate wafer crumbs
½ cup chopped pecans or walnuts
1 teaspoon vanilla extract
1 quart coffee ice cream, softened
1 cup whipping cream
⅓ cup powdered sugar
Grated chocolate
Commercial fudge sauce

Beat egg whites (at room temperature) until frothy; add baking powder, beating slightly. Gradually add sugar and salt; continue beating until stiff and glossy. Fold in chocolate wafer crumbs, pecans, and vanilla.

Spoon meringue into a buttered 9-inch piepan; use spoon to shape meringue into a pie shell, swirling sides high. Bake at 350° for 30 minutes; cool.

Spread ice cream evenly over meringue crust; cover and freeze overnight.

Combine whipping cream and powdered sugar, beating until light and fluffy; spread on pie. Garnish with grated chocolate; freeze until firm.

Let pie stand at room temperature 10 minutes before slicing. Spoon fudge sauce over each serving. Yield: one 9-inch pie.

Note: This pie is thick and rich. It will easily yield 8 servings.

Guests enjoy adding their own toppings of chili, green onion, cheese, and bacon to fluffy baked potatoes.

Shape your cheese mixture into a Christmas tree instead of the traditional ball.

CHILI-TOPPED POTATOES

8 large baking potatoes
Vegetable oil
1 pound ground beef
1 (28-ounce) can tomatoes, undrained
1 cup water
1 (16-ounce) can kidney beans, undrained
1 (6-ounce) can tomato paste
2 to 3 stalks celery, chopped
1 green pepper, chopped
1 large onion, chopped
1 to 2 tablespoons chili powder
Salt and pepper to taste
Crumbled cooked bacon
Shredded Cheddar cheese
Chopped green onions

Wash potatoes and rub with oil. Bake at 400° for 1 hour or until soft when pierced with a fork.

Cook ground beef in a Dutch oven until browned, stirring to crumble. Drain off pan drippings. Stir in next 9 ingredients; simmer, uncovered, 45 minutes or until thickened, stirring occasionally.

Split tops of potatoes lengthwise, and fluff pulp with a fork. Spoon topping over potatoes. Sprinkle with bacon, cheese, and green onions. Yield: 8 servings.

CHEESE TREE

1 (8-ounce) package extra sharp Cheddar
    cheese, shredded
1 (8-ounce) package medium Cheddar
    cheese, shredded
¼ cup grated onion
½ cup mayonnaise
½ teaspoon red pepper
1 cup chopped fresh parsley
Fresh cranberries

Combine first 5 ingredients, mixing well. Shape into a cone. Press chopped parsley onto tree to cover all surfaces. Place cranberries on tree as ornaments. Serve with crackers. Yield: 1 cheese tree.

VEGETABLE PITAS

1 large cucumber
1 large yellow squash
1 large carrot, scraped and grated
2½ cups alfalfa sprouts
½ cup crumbled feta cheese
¼ cup commercial Italian salad dressing
Leaf lettuce
4 (6-inch) whole wheat pocket bread
   rounds, cut in half

Cut cucumber and squash in half lengthwise; slice thinly. Combine cucumber,
squash, and next 4 ingredients; toss well.
   Place lettuce leaf in each pocket bread
half; fill with sandwich mixture. Yield: 8
servings.
   Note: If vegetable mixture is made ahead
and allowed to stand, drain mixture well before assembling sandwiches.

CHRISTMAS FORTUNE COOKIES

1 pound butter, softened
1 cup sugar
6 cups all-purpose flour
Royal Icing

Cream butter; gradually add sugar, beating
until light and fluffy. Add flour to creamed
mixture, mixing well (dough will be dry).
   Working with a small amount of dough at
a time, roll dough out on an unfloured board
to ⅛-inch thickness, using a floured rolling
pin. Cut out with a 2½-inch doughnut cut-
ter, reserving centers. Place cookies on ungreased cookie sheets; reroll holes.
   Bake at 400° for 5 to 7 minutes or until
lightly browned (watch closely to prevent
over-browning). Remove to wire racks to
cool.
   Prepare 4½ dozen fortunes on 4- x 1-inch
strips of paper; fold the paper strips in half
lengthwise, and set aside.
   Prepare a decorating bag with green icing
and metal decorating tip No. 75. Prepare another decorating bag with red icing and tip
No. 3. Pipe green leaves using tip No. 75
on top of half the cookies. Pipe small holly

berries around leaves using red icing and
metal tip No. 3. Pipe bows on cookies using
red icing and tip No. 3 or 44. Set cookies
aside to dry.
   Pipe a small strip of red icing at top and
bottom of back side of remaining cookies.
Lay a fortune across center of cookies, not
touching icing. Top with decorated cookies,
top side up. Set cookies aside to dry. Yield:
4½ dozen.

Royal Icing:

3 egg whites
½ teaspoon cream of tartar
1 (16-ounce) package powdered sugar
Red and green paste food coloring

Combine egg whites (at room temperature)
and cream of tartar in a large mixing bowl.
Beat at medium speed of electric mixer until
frothy. Gradually add powdered sugar, mixing well. Beat for 5 to 7 minutes. Color
about one-fourth of the icing red, and color
remaining icing green. Yield: about 2 cups.
   Note: Icing dries very quickly; keep covered at all times with plastic wrap.

Christmas Fortune Cookies can be the highlight of your
party. Personalize a fortune for each guest .

CHRISTMAS DINNER

ROAST TURKEY
OLD-FASHIONED CORNBREAD DRESSING
SAUSAGE-CRACKER DRESSING
OYSTER-BREAD DRESSING
FESTIVE CRANBERRY SALAD
ORANGE-SWEET POTATO CUPS
EASY BUTTERMILK ROLLS
ENGLISH PEA CASSEROLE
GIBLET GRAVY
PICKLED CARROTS
FAVORITE PUMPKIN PIE

When the family gathers around the table for Christmas dinner, it's a time for love, for remembering years past, and for the meal that is traditional in your family. Many families serve the same basic meal year after year, usually consisting of turkey and all the trimmings. If your family insists on this meal, yet your recipes could use a little excitement, try these delicious variations on the customary theme.

ROAST TURKEY
1 (12- to 14-pound) turkey
Salt
Melted butter, margarine, or vegetable oil
Fresh parsley sprigs
Purple grapes
Orange wedges

Remove giblets and rinse turkey thoroughly with cold water; pat dry. Sprinkle cavity with salt. Tie ends of legs to tail with cord or string, or tuck them under flap of skin around tail. Lift wingtips up and over back so they are tucked under bird.

The traditional Christmas dinner is still the favorite. Clockwise from front: Roast Turkey, Festive Cranberry Salad, Sausage-Cracker Dressing, English Pea Casserole, Giblet Gravy, Orange-Sweet Potato Cups, Easy Buttermilk Rolls, Pickled Carrots.

Brush entire bird with melted butter; place on a roasting rack, breast side up. Insert a meat thermometer in breast or meaty part of thigh, making sure it does not touch bone. Bake at 325° until meat thermometer reaches 185° (about 4½ to 5 hours). If turkey starts to brown too much, cover loosely with aluminum foil.

When turkey is two-thirds done, cut the cord or band of skin holding the drumstick ends to the tail; this will ensure that the inside of the thighs is cooked. Turkey is done when drumsticks are easy to move up and down. Let stand 15 minutes before carving. Garnish with parsley, grapes, and orange wedges. Yield: 20 to 24 servings.

Note: Never stuff a turkey the night before cooking. Immediately before roasting, stuff dressing into cavity of turkey, and close cavity with skewers. Then tie ends of legs as directed above.

Stuffed turkeys require about 5 minutes more cooking per pound. Be sure to remove stuffing before storing leftover turkey in the refrigerator.

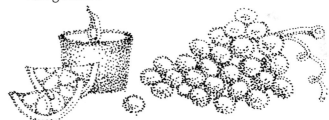

OLD-FASHIONED CORNBREAD DRESSING
4 cups crumbled cornbread
1 cup saltine cracker crumbs
1 cup crumbled white bread
1 teaspoon poultry seasoning
½ teaspoon salt
½ teaspoon rubbed sage
½ teaspoon pepper
½ teaspoon celery salt
½ cup chopped onion
3 hard-cooked eggs, chopped
2 to 2½ cups chicken or turkey broth

Combine all ingredients; mix well. Stuff turkey lightly or place in a greased 3-quart casserole; bake at 350° for 30 minutes or until done. Yield: 8 to 10 servings.

SAUSAGE-CRACKER DRESSING

About 1½ pounds giblets
1 pound mild bulk pork sausage
½ cup butter or margarine
4 large celery stalks, diced
1 large onion, diced
10 cups coarsely broken saltine crackers
1 to 1¼ cups milk
¾ teaspoon dried whole rosemary
½ teaspoon pepper
3 eggs, beaten
Celery leaves (optional)
Tomato rose (optional)

Place giblets in a Dutch oven; cover with water and bring to a boil. Cover, reduce heat, and simmer 30 minutes or until giblets are tender. Drain, reserving 1¾ cups broth. Chop meat.

Brown sausage in a large skillet, stirring to crumble; remove sausage with a slotted spoon. Add butter to drippings in skillet; cook over low heat until butter melts. Stir in celery and onion; sauté until vegetables are tender.

Combine reserved giblet broth, chopped giblets, sausage, sautéed vegetables, and next 5 ingredients in a large bowl; stir well. Stuff turkey lightly or place in a greased 13- x 9- x 2-inch baking dish. Bake at 350° for 30 to 35 minutes. Garnish with celery leaves and tomato rose. Yield: 10 servings.

To make a tomato rose, peel a paper-thin continuous strip about ¾-inch wide. Beginning at first portion cut, with flesh side inward, coil tightly to form center; coil more loosely to form outer petals.

OYSTER-BREAD DRESSING

1 (1-pound) loaf French bread
¼ pound chicken gizzards
3 cups water
1 cup finely chopped onion
¼ cup finely chopped celery
¼ cup finely chopped green pepper
1 bunch green onions, finely chopped
1 bunch fresh parsley, finely chopped
2 cloves garlic, crushed
¼ cup butter or margarine
½ pound ground lean beef
¼ pound ground pork
¼ pound chicken livers, finely chopped
1 teaspoon instant-blending flour
½ teaspoon salt
¼ teaspoon black pepper
¼ teaspoon ground red pepper
2 dashes of hot sauce
2½ pints oysters, undrained

Cut bread in half lengthwise and place cut side up on a baking sheet; bake at 350° for 15 to 20 minutes or until lightly browned. Cool. Tear bread into about 1-inch pieces. Place in a large bowl, and set aside.

Place gizzards and 3 cups of water in a saucepan; cover and cook over medium heat 45 minutes or until tender. Remove gizzards, reserving 1½ cups broth. Finely chop gizzards; set aside.

Sauté vegetables, parsley, and garlic in butter in a large skillet. Add gizzards, ground beef, pork, and livers; cook over medium-high heat until meat is no longer pink, stirring to crumble meat. Add reserved chicken broth; reduce heat to low, and simmer 30 minutes or until broth has been reduced to about ½ cup. Stir in flour and seasonings; simmer 10 minutes.

Spoon mixture over bread. Cut oysters in half; add oysters and oyster liquid to bread mixture. Stir until well combined. Stuff turkey lightly or spoon mixture into a well-greased 3-quart casserole. Bake at 350° for 20 minutes or until thoroughly heated. Yield: 8 servings.

FESTIVE CRANBERRY SALAD

4 cups fresh cranberries
1 large orange, unpeeled, seeded, and
  ground
1 cup sugar
1 envelope unflavored gelatin
⅓ cup cold water
⅔ cup boiling water
1 (3-ounce) package lemon-flavored
  gelatin
1 (15-ounce) can crushed pineapple,
  undrained
1 cup chopped walnuts
½ cup diced celery
Lettuce leaves
Mayonnaise

Set aside a few cranberries for garnish.
Grind remaining cranberries. Combine the
ground cranberries, orange, and sugar; cover
and chill 1 hour.

Soften unflavored gelatin in cold water; let
stand 1 minute. Stir in boiling water and
lemon-flavored gelatin; stir until gelatin dissolves. Gently stir in cranberry mixture,
pineapple, walnuts, and celery. Spoon mixture into a 6-cup mold; chill until firm. Un-
mold on lettuce-lined serving plate. Line
center ring with lettuce; spoon mayonnaise
in center. Top with reserved cranberries.
Yield: 8 servings.

ORANGE-SWEET POTATO CUPS

8 large oranges
4 large sweet potatoes
1 cup sugar
2 eggs
1 teaspoon vanilla extract
⅓ cup milk
½ cup butter or margarine, softened
½ cup firmly packed brown sugar
2½ tablespoons all-purpose flour
½ cup finely chopped walnuts
2 tablespoons butter or margarine,
  softened
Fresh parsley sprigs (optional)

Cut a thin slice from bottom of oranges so
they will not roll. Cut a ¾-inch slice from top
of each orange. Gently remove pulp, leaving
shells intact (reserve pulp for other uses). Set
aside.

Cook sweet potatoes in boiling water 25 to
30 minutes or until tender. Let cool to touch;
peel and mash.

Combine the sweet potatoes, sugar, eggs,
vanilla, milk, and ½ cup butter; beat with
electric mixer until smooth. Spoon into the
orange cups. Place orange cups in a baking
pan.

Combine brown sugar, flour, walnuts, and
2 tablespoons butter; sprinkle mixture over
top of orange cups. Bake at 350° for 10 to
15 minutes. Arrange on platter and garnish
with parsley. Yield: 8 servings.

EASY BUTTERMILK ROLLS

4 to 4½ cups all-purpose flour, divided
2 packages dry yeast
3 tablespoons sugar
1 teaspoon salt
½ teaspoon baking soda
1¼ cups buttermilk
½ cup water
½ cup shortening

Combine 1½ cups flour, yeast, sugar, salt,
and soda in a large bowl, mixing well. Combine buttermilk, water, and shortening in a
small saucepan; place over low heat until
very warm (120° to 130°). Gradually add the
milk mixture to dry ingredients, mixing at
low speed of an electric mixer; then beat 3
minutes on medium speed. Stir in remaining
flour.

Turn dough out onto a lightly floured surface, and knead until smooth and elastic
(about 5 minutes).

Place dough in a greased bowl; turn to
grease top. Cover and let rise in a warm
place (85°), free from drafts, 45 minutes or
until doubled in bulk.

Punch dough down and shape into 1½-
inch balls; place on a greased 15- x 10- x
1-inch jellyroll pan. Let rise in a warm place
(85°), free from drafts, for 35 minutes or until
doubled in bulk. Bake at 400° for 18 to 20
minutes. Yield: 2 dozen.

ENGLISH PEA CASSEROLE

2 (17-ounce) cans English peas, drained
1 (10¾-ounce) can cream of mushroom
  soup, undiluted
1 (2-ounce) jar diced pimiento, undrained
4 hard-cooked eggs, chopped
1 (2.8-ounce) can fried onion rings, divided
1½ cups (6 ounces) shredded Cheddar
  cheese, divided
Fresh parsley sprigs

Combine first 4 ingredients and half of
onion rings, mixing well. Spoon half of pea
mixture into a lightly greased 2-quart baking
dish. Top with half of cheese. Spoon remaining pea mixture over cheese, and top with
remaining cheese. Sprinkle remaining onion
rings over top. Bake, uncovered, at 350° for
15 to 20 minutes or until thoroughly heated.
Garnish with parsley. Yield: 8 servings.

GIBLET GRAVY

Giblets from 1 turkey
Turkey neck
2 cups chicken broth
1 medium onion, chopped
1 cup chopped celery
½ teaspoon poultry seasoning
½ cup cornbread dressing
Salt and pepper to taste
2 hard-cooked eggs, sliced

Cook giblets and turkey neck in chicken
broth until tender and done. Remove giblets
and neck from broth; cool. Remove meat
from neck and discard bones; chop giblets
and return all meat to broth.
Add onion, celery, poultry seasoning, and
dressing to broth mixture; cook until vegetables are tender. Stir in salt, pepper, and egg
slices. If thicker gravy is desired, add more
dressing. Yield: about 2 cups.
Note: All-purpose flour may be used instead of dressing to thicken gravy. Dissolve 2
tablespoons flour in small amount of water,
and stir into broth.

PICKLED CARROTS

2 pounds carrots, peeled and cut into 3- x
  ¼-inch strips
1½ cups sugar
1½ cups vinegar
1½ cups water
¼ cup whole mustard seeds
3 (½-inch) sticks cinnamon
3 whole cloves

Cook carrots, covered, about 15 minutes
in a small amount of boiling, salted water.
Drain carrots and place in a glass or plastic
container.
Combine remaining ingredients in a saucepan; bring to a boil and simmer 20 minutes.
Pour over carrots; toss well. Cover tightly; then
refrigerate overnight. Yield: 8 to 10 servings.
Note: Carrots may be stored in refrigerator
2 weeks. Liquid may be reused; cook additional carrots as directed.

FAVORITE PUMPKIN PIE

2 cups cooked, mashed pumpkin
1 cup firmly packed brown sugar
½ cup butter or margarine, softened
2 eggs, separated
½ teaspoon ground ginger
½ teaspoon ground cinnamon
½ teaspoon ground nutmeg
¼ teaspoon salt
½ cup evaporated milk
¼ cup sugar
1 unbaked 10-inch pastry shell
Whipped topping (optional)

Combine pumpkin, brown sugar, butter,
egg yolks, spices, and salt in a large mixing
bowl; beat until light and fluffy. Add evaporated milk; mix only until combined.
Beat egg whites (at room temperature)
until foamy; gradually add sugar, beating
until stiff. Fold into pumpkin mixture. Pour
filling into pastry shell. Bake at 400° for 10
minutes; reduce heat to 350° and bake an
additional 45 to 50 minutes or until set.
Cool. Top with whipped topping, if desired.
Yield: one 10-inch pie.

PATTERNS

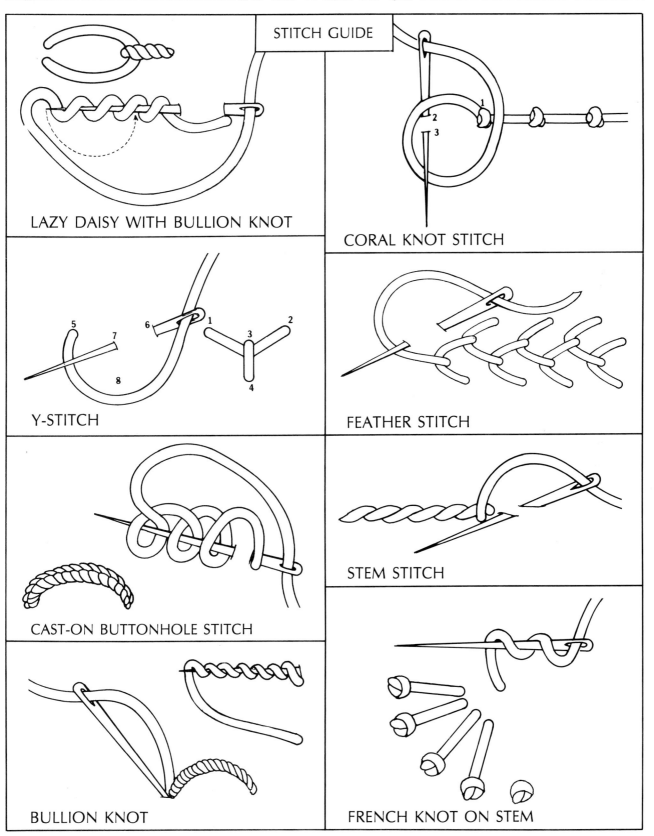

STITCH GUIDE

LAZY DAISY WITH BULLION KNOT

CORAL KNOT STITCH

Y-STITCH

FEATHER STITCH

CAST-ON BUTTONHOLE STITCH

STEM STITCH

BULLION KNOT

FRENCH KNOT ON STEM

INITIAL CHART

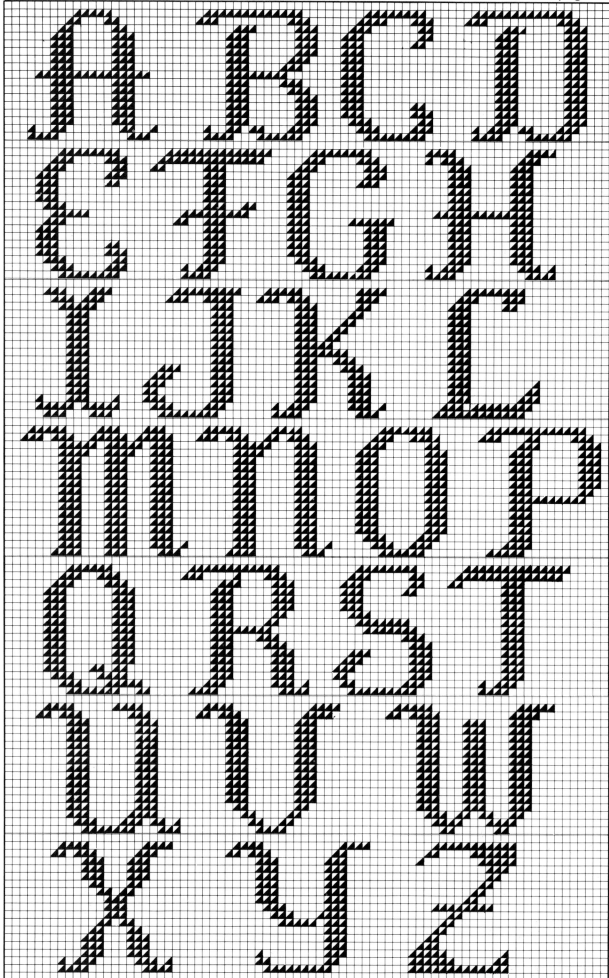

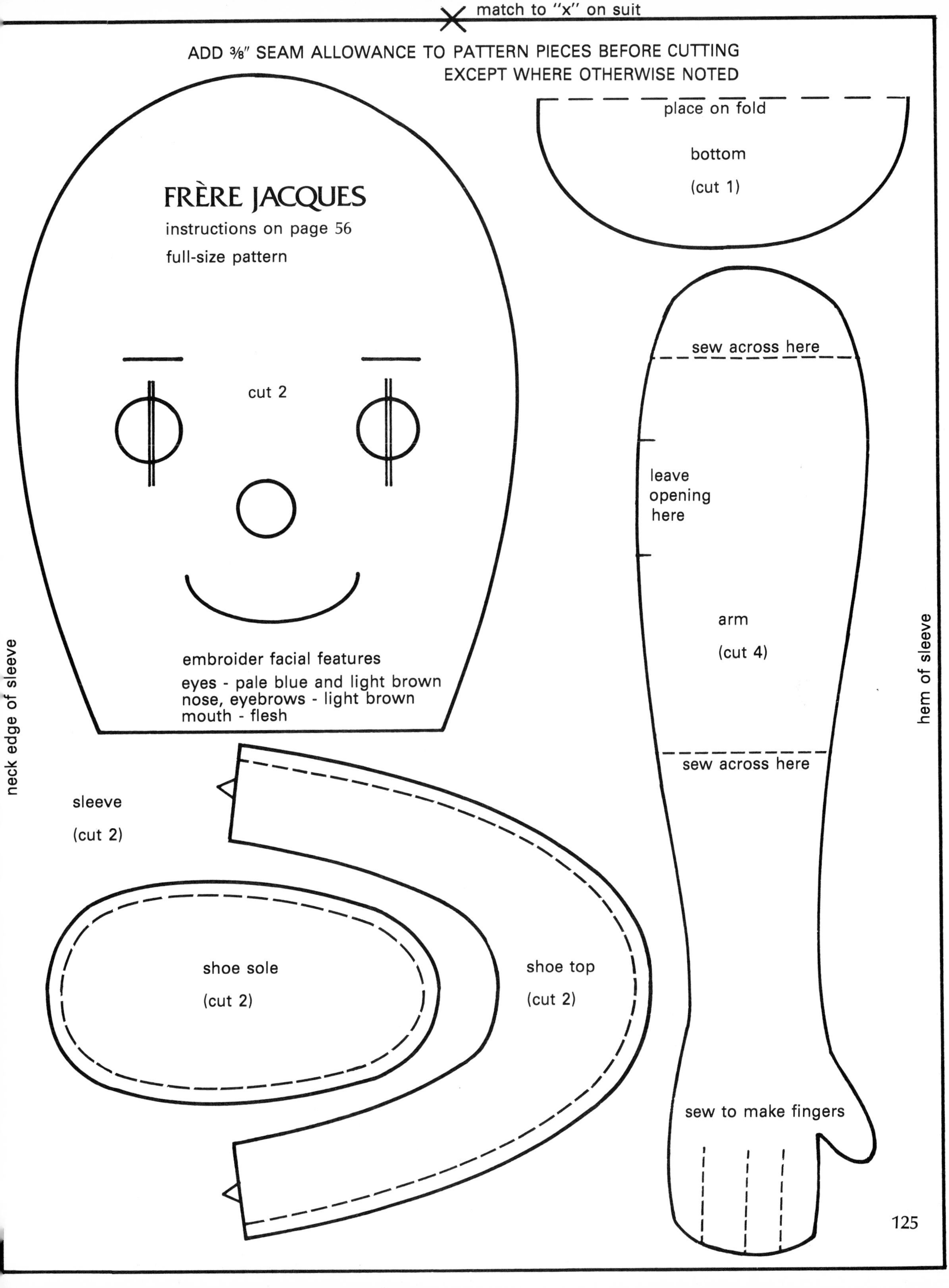
match to "x" on suit
ADD ⅜" SEAM ALLOWANCE TO PATTERN PIECES BEFORE CUTTING
EXCEPT WHERE OTHERWISE NOTED
FRÈRE JACQUES
instructions on page 56
full-size pattern
cut 2
embroider facial features
eyes - pale blue and light brown
nose, eyebrows - light brown
mouth - flesh
place on fold
bottom
(cut 1)
sew across here
leave
opening
here
arm
(cut 4)
sew across here
sew to make fingers
hem of sleeve
neck edge of sleeve
sleeve
(cut 2)
shoe sole
(cut 2)
shoe top
(cut 2)

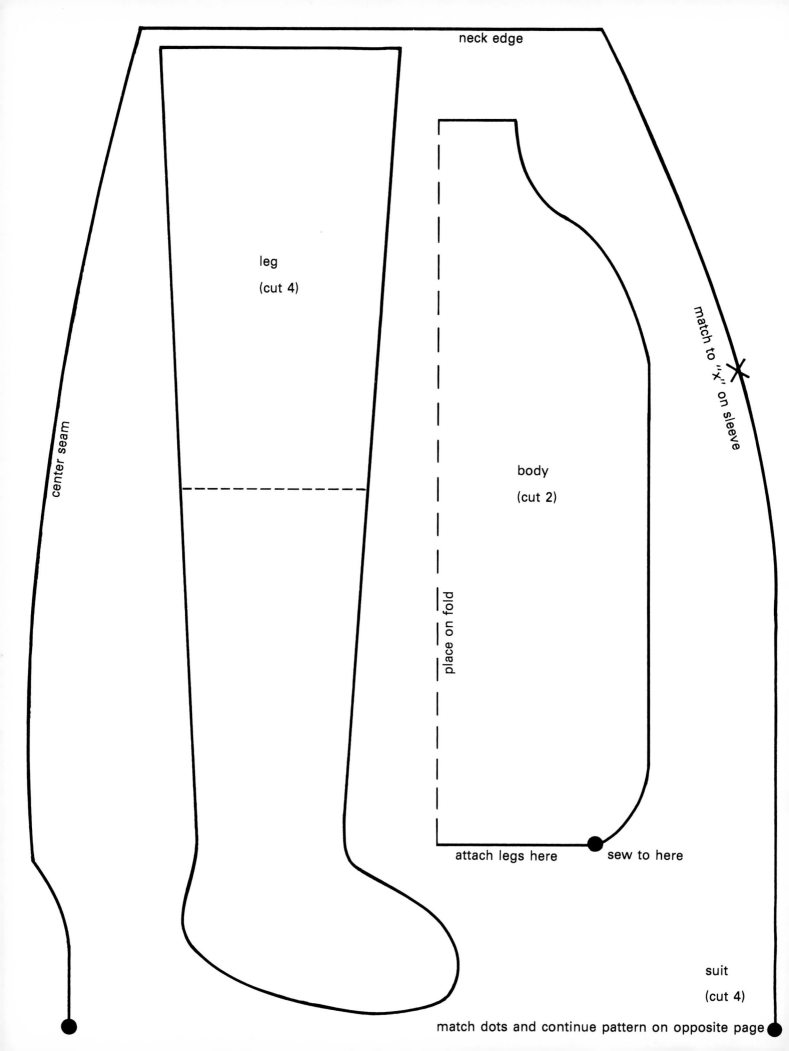

neck edge

leg

(cut 4)

center seam

match to "x" on sleeve

body

(cut 2)

place on fold

attach legs here · sew to here

suit

(cut 4)

match dots and continue pattern on opposite page

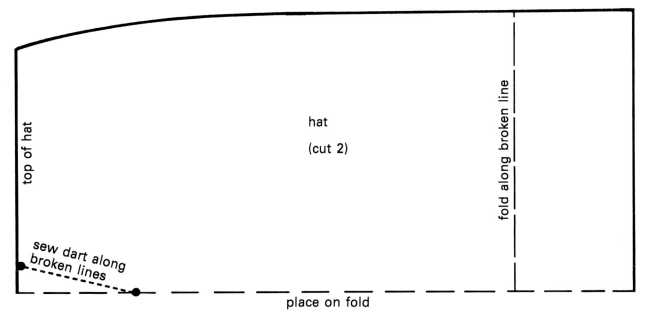

top of hat

hat

(cut 2)

fold along broken line

sew dart along
broken lines

place on fold

match dots and continue pattern on opposite page

suit

(cut 4)

FRÈRE JACQUES
(continued)

instructions on page 56
full-size pattern

"BUSTER BEAR"
COLLAGE
instructions on page 26
full-size pattern

cut all pieces from
your choice of fabrics

draw mouth
with fine-point
marking pen

Cut 1:
 bear shape
 vest
 nose
 bow tie
 collar
 large heart
 wreath
 bow for wreath
 horse
 tail for horse
 rocker for horse
 small package
 large package

Cut 2:
 eyes
 ear pieces

Cut 3:
 small hearts

128

match "x"s and continue pattern on opposite page

make bows from embroidery floss

match "x"s and continue pattern on opposite page

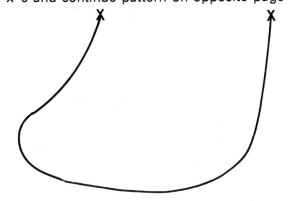

Snowman box
(cut 4 for each box)
cut along solid lines

nail together at sides

side view of box

side view of box

nail lath
strips on bottom

A WINTER WONDERLAND
instructions on page 6 and 7
full-size pattern

red

green

paint as indicated
in photograph

130

front view

back view

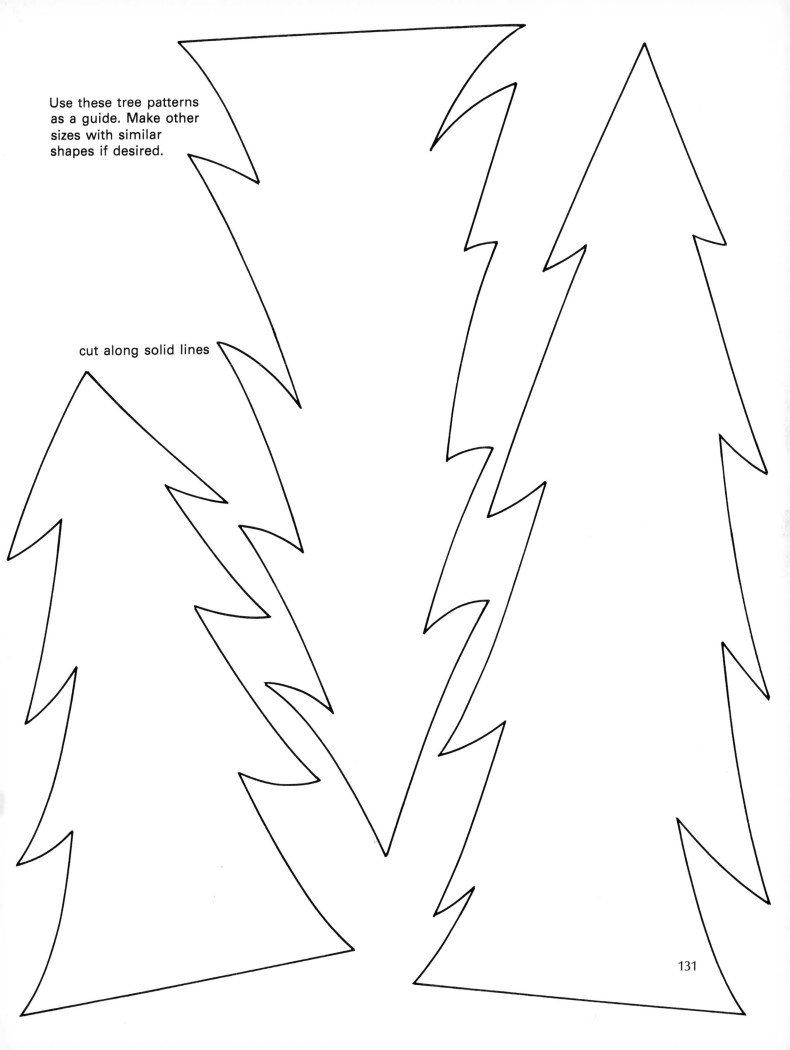

Use these tree patterns as a guide. Make other sizes with similar shapes if desired.

cut along solid lines

131

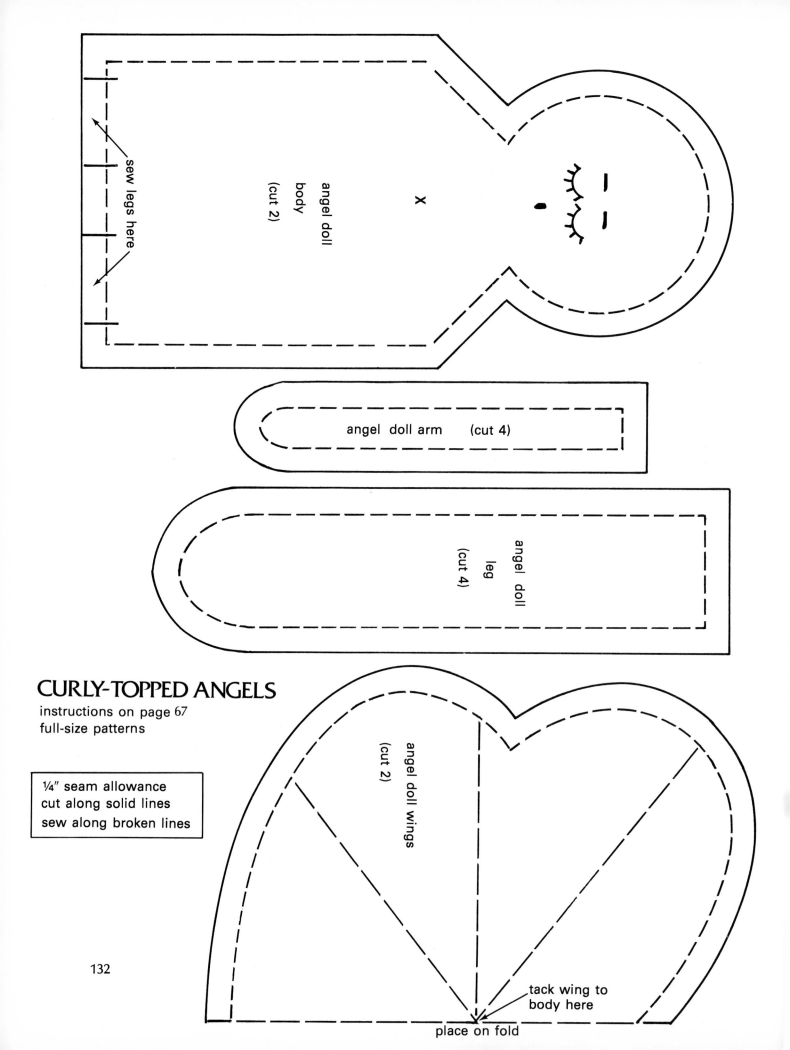

sew legs here

angel doll
body
(cut 2)

X

angel doll arm   (cut 4)

angel doll
leg
(cut 4)

CURLY-TOPPED ANGELS

instructions on page 67
full-size patterns

¼″ seam allowance
cut along solid lines
sew along broken lines

angel doll wings
(cut 2)

tack wing to
body here

place on fold

132

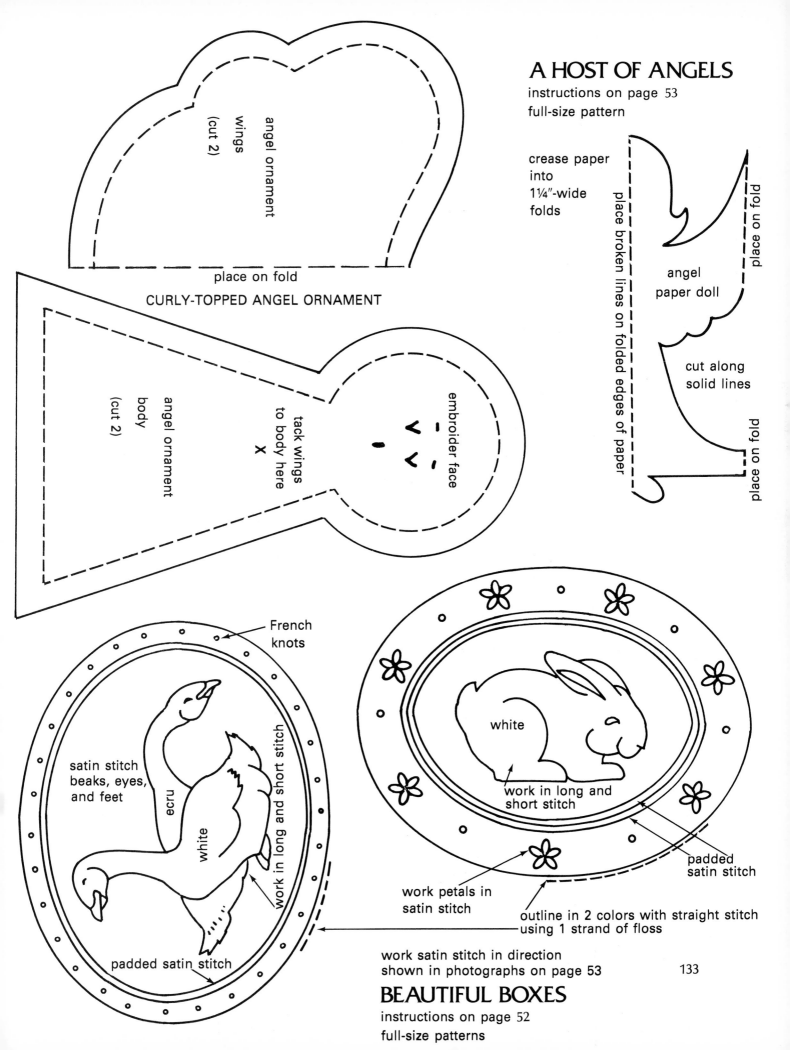

angel ornament
wings
(cut 2)

place on fold

CURLY-TOPPED ANGEL ORNAMENT

angel ornament
body
(cut 2)

tack wings
to body here
X

embroider face

A HOST OF ANGELS
instructions on page 53
full-size pattern

crease paper
into
1¼"-wide
folds

angel
paper doll

cut along
solid lines

place broken lines on folded edges of paper

place on fold

place on fold

place on fold

French
knots

satin stitch
beaks, eyes,
and feet

ecru

white

work in long and short stitch

padded satin stitch

white

work in long and
short stitch

work petals in
satin stitch

padded
satin stitch

outline in 2 colors with straight stitch
using 1 strand of floss

work satin stitch in direction
shown in photographs on page 53

133

BEAUTIFUL BOXES
instructions on page 52
full-size patterns

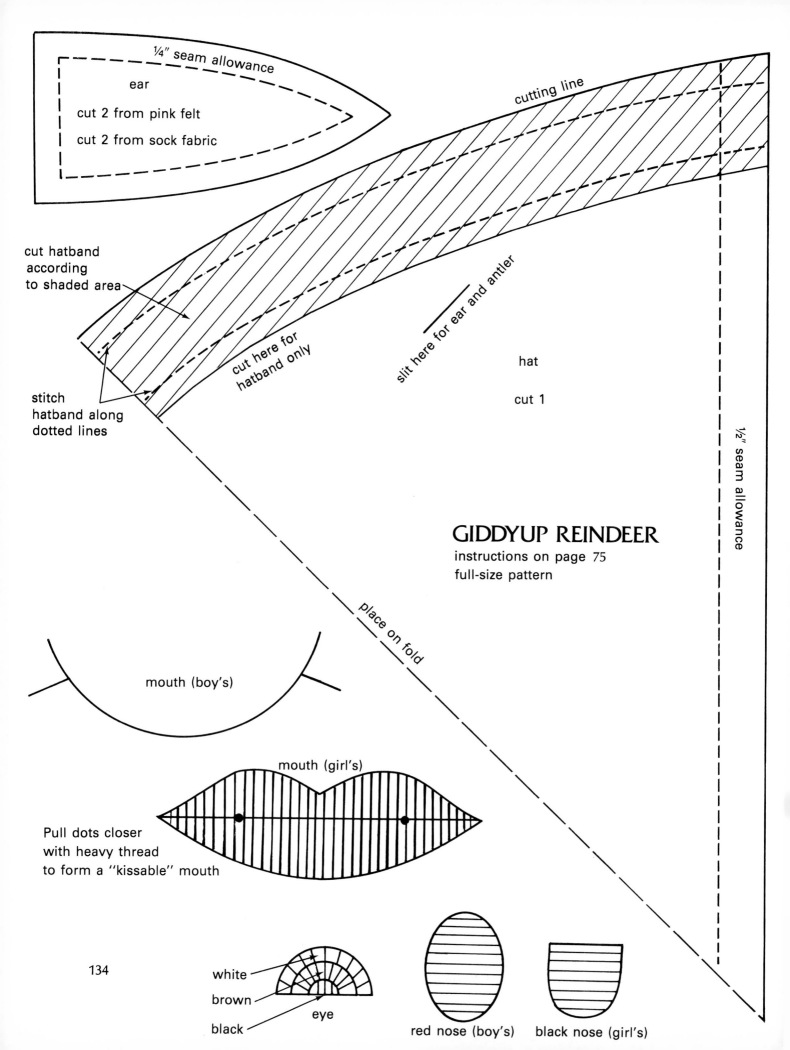

¼" seam allowance

ear

cut 2 from pink felt

cut 2 from sock fabric

cutting line

cut hatband
according
to shaded area

cut here for
hatband only

slit here for ear and antler

hat

cut 1

stitch
hatband along
dotted lines

½" seam allowance

GIDDYUP REINDEER
instructions on page 75
full-size pattern

place on fold

mouth (boy's)

mouth (girl's)

Pull dots closer
with heavy thread
to form a "kissable" mouth

134

white

brown

black

eye

red nose (boy's)

black nose (girl's)

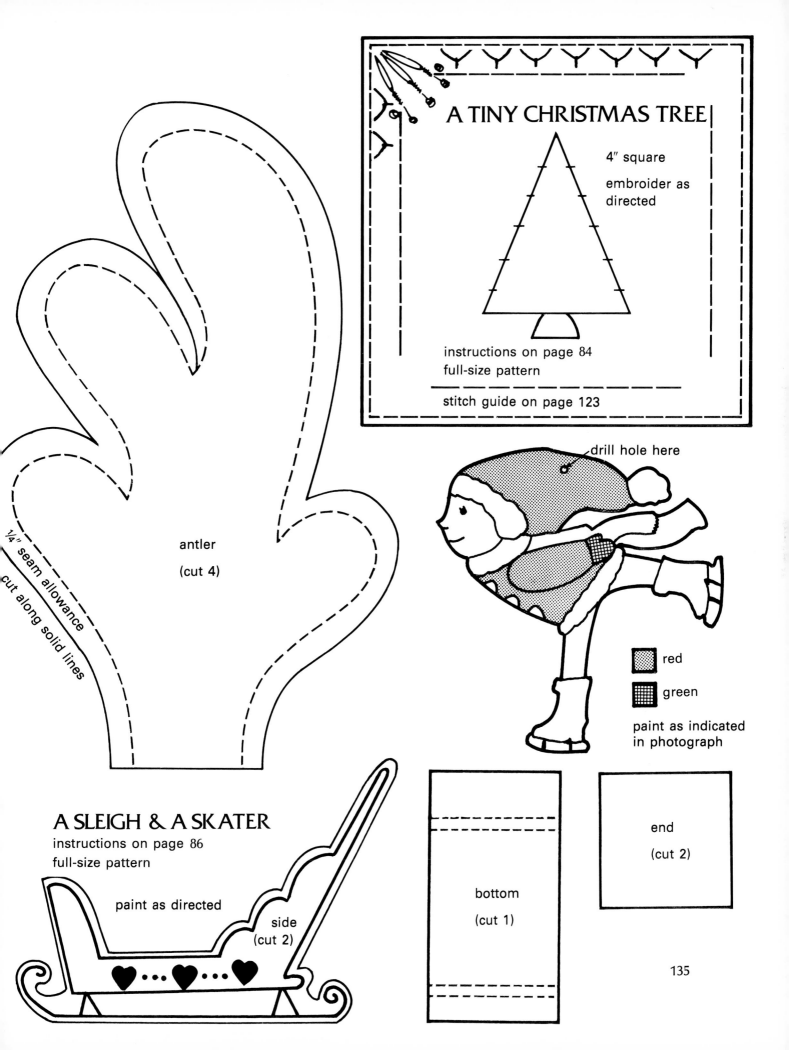

A TINY CHRISTMAS TREE

4" square

embroider as directed

instructions on page 84
full-size pattern

stitch guide on page 123

antler
(cut 4)

¼" seam allowance
cut along solid lines

drill hole here

▨ red

▦ green

paint as indicated
in photograph

A SLEIGH & A SKATER

instructions on page 86
full-size pattern

paint as directed

side
(cut 2)

bottom
(cut 1)

end
(cut 2)

135

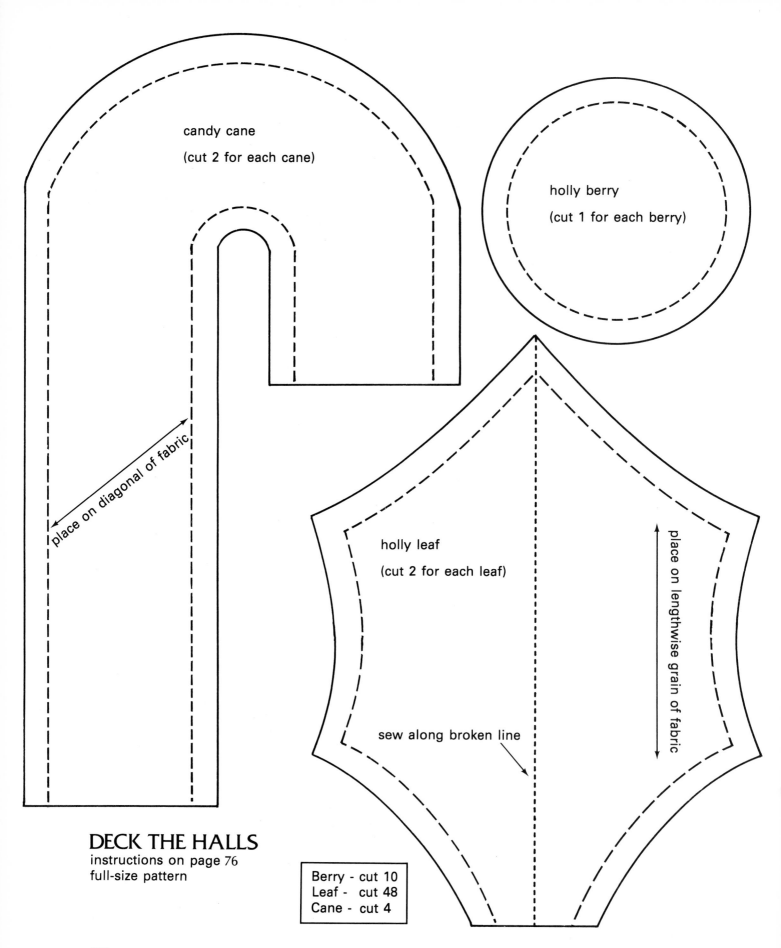

candy cane

(cut 2 for each cane)

place on diagonal of fabric

holly berry

(cut 1 for each berry)

holly leaf

(cut 2 for each leaf)

sew along broken line

place on lengthwise grain of fabric

DECK THE HALLS
instructions on page 76
full-size pattern

Berry - cut 10
Leaf - cut 48
Cane - cut 4

MERRY MERRY MOOSE

instructions on page 73
full-size pattern

cut along solid lines

sew along broken lines

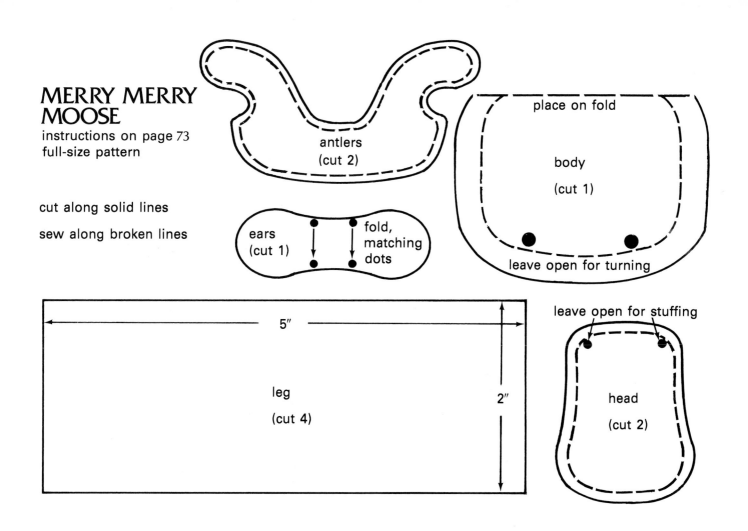

antlers
(cut 2)

ears
(cut 1)

fold,
matching
dots

place on fold

body
(cut 1)

leave open for turning

leave open for stuffing

head
(cut 2)

5"

2"

leg
(cut 4)

LUCY LAMBCHOP

instructions on page 72
full-size pattern

embroider face
with black floss

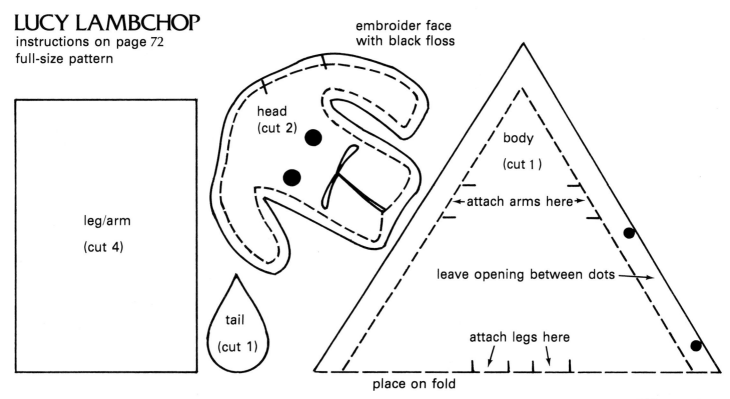

leg/arm
(cut 4)

head
(cut 2)

tail
(cut 1)

body
(cut 1)

←attach arms here→

leave opening between dots →

attach legs here

place on fold

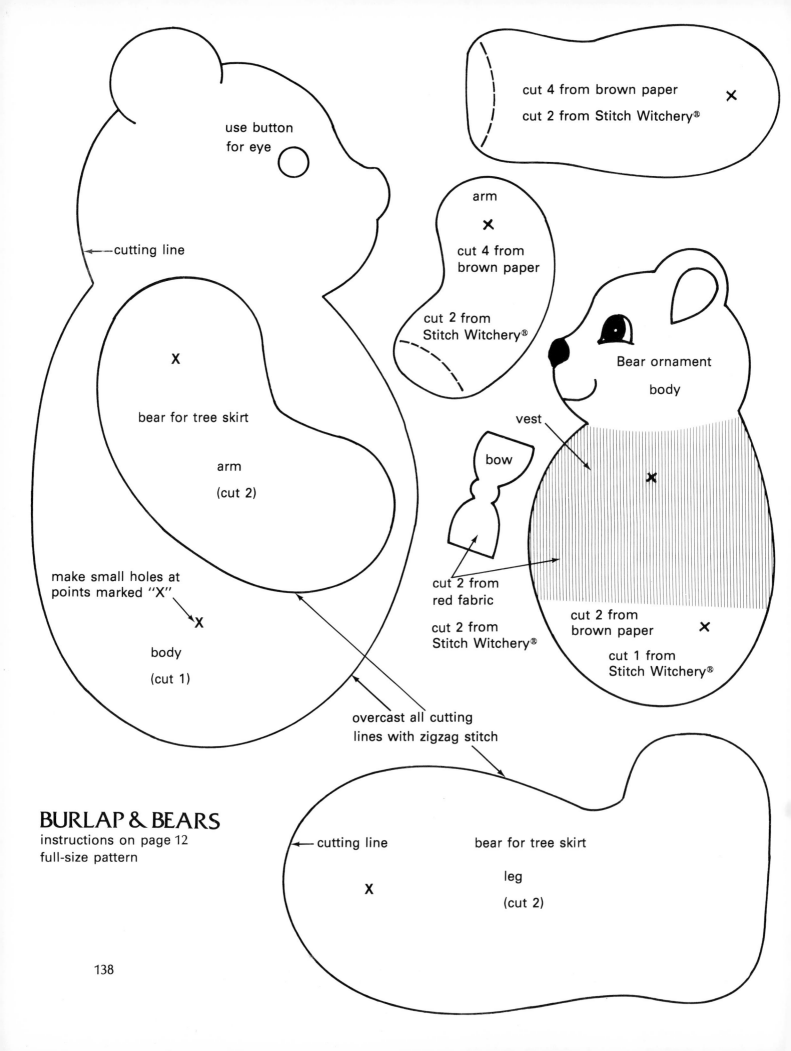

use button for eye

cut 4 from brown paper
cut 2 from Stitch Witchery®

← cutting line

arm
✗
cut 4 from brown paper

cut 2 from Stitch Witchery®

Bear ornament
body

vest

bow

✗

bear for tree skirt

arm
(cut 2)

cut 2 from red fabric

cut 2 from Stitch Witchery®

cut 2 from brown paper

cut 1 from Stitch Witchery®

make small holes at points marked "X"
→✗

body
(cut 1)

overcast all cutting lines with zigzag stitch

BURLAP & BEARS
instructions on page 12
full-size pattern

← cutting line

bear for tree skirt

leg
(cut 2)

✗

138

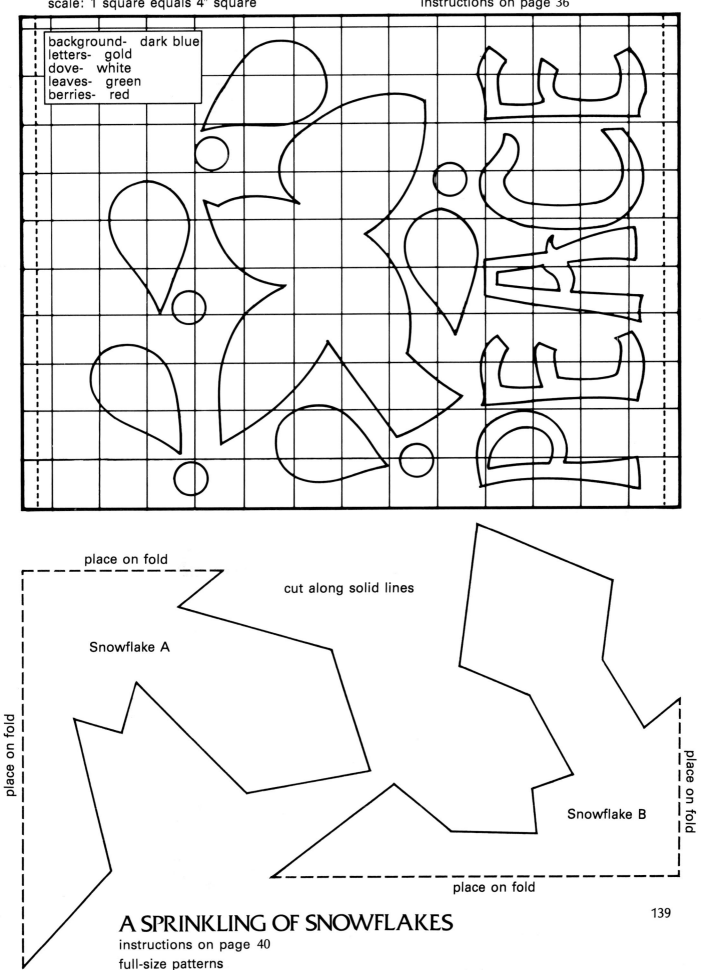

scale: 1 square equals 4″ square

background-   dark blue
letters-   gold
dove-   white
leaves-   green
berries-   red

place on fold

cut along solid lines

Snowflake A

place on fold

place on fold

Snowflake B

place on fold

139

A SPRINKLING OF SNOWFLAKES

instructions on page 40

full-size patterns

MRS. SANTA RECIPE HOLDER

instructions on page 60
full-size pattern

paint as indicated in photograph

Color Key

▦ red
▦ green

X
X

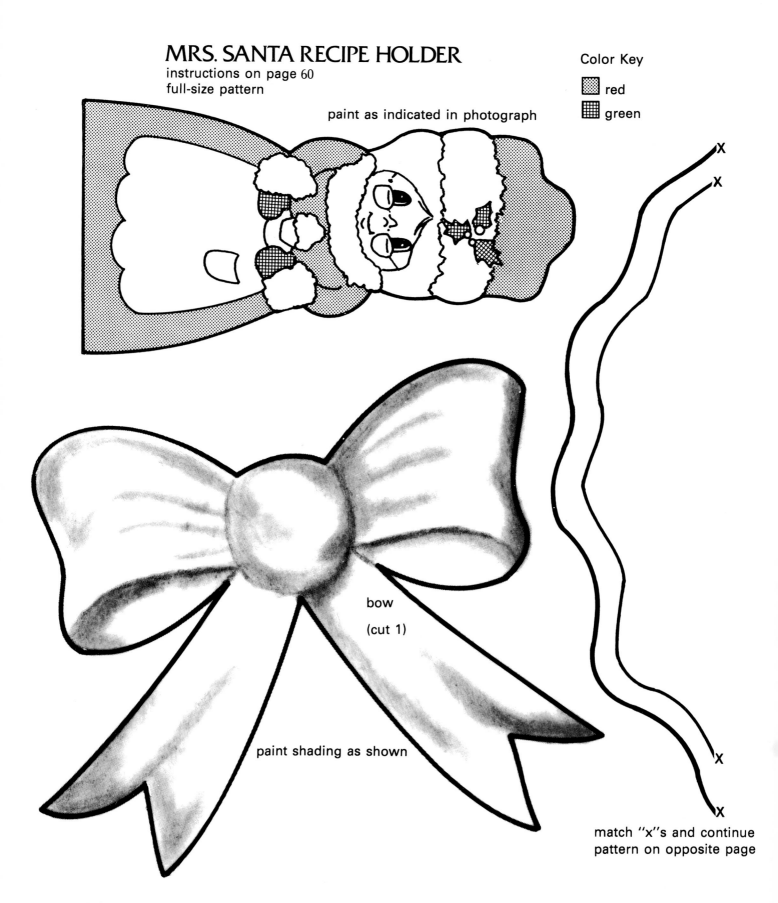

bow

(cut 1)

paint shading as shown

X
X
X

match ''x''s and continue
pattern on opposite page

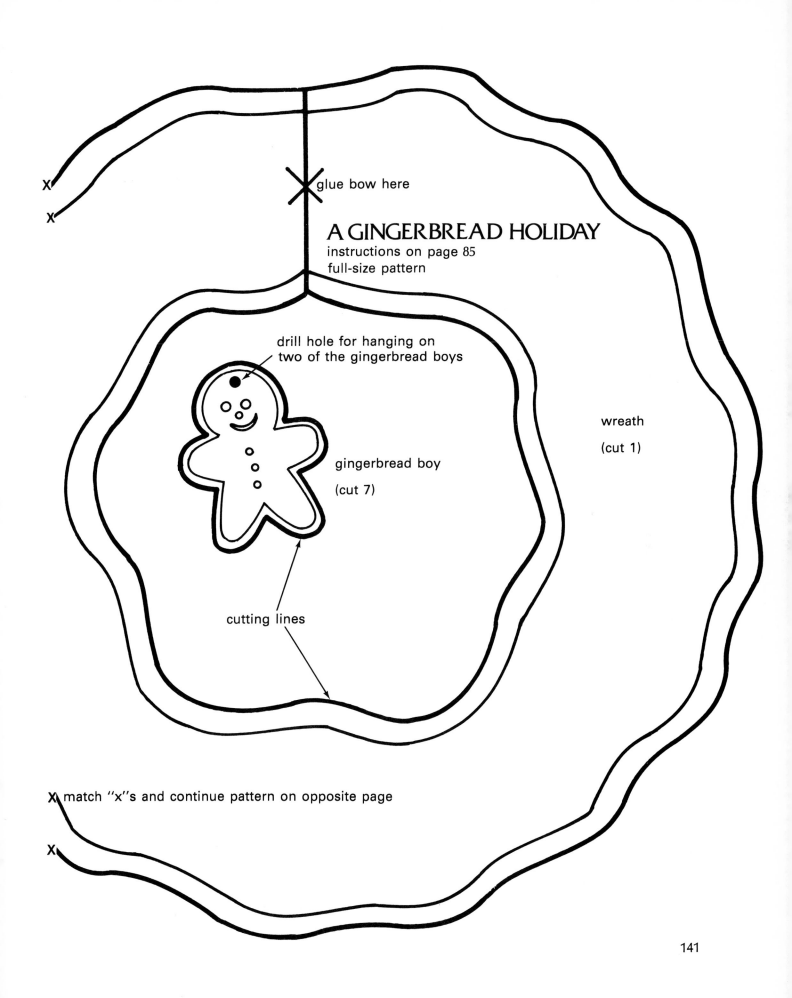

X

X

X glue bow here

A GINGERBREAD HOLIDAY
instructions on page 85
full-size pattern

drill hole for hanging on
two of the gingerbread boys

wreath

(cut 1)

gingerbread boy

(cut 7)

cutting lines

X match "x"s and continue pattern on opposite page

X

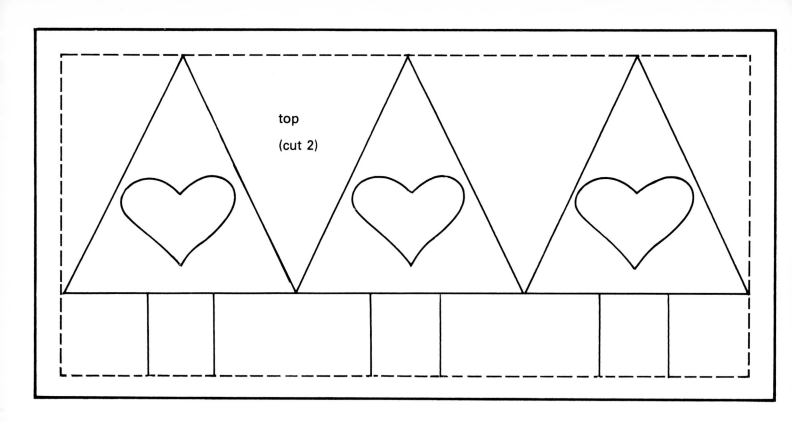

top
(cut 2)

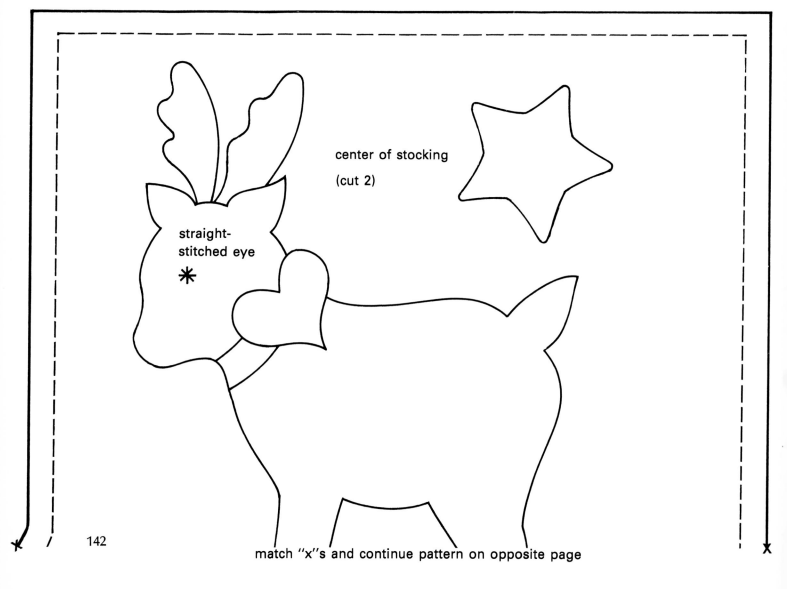

center of stocking

(cut 2)

straight-
stitched eye

✳

match "x"s and continue pattern on opposite page

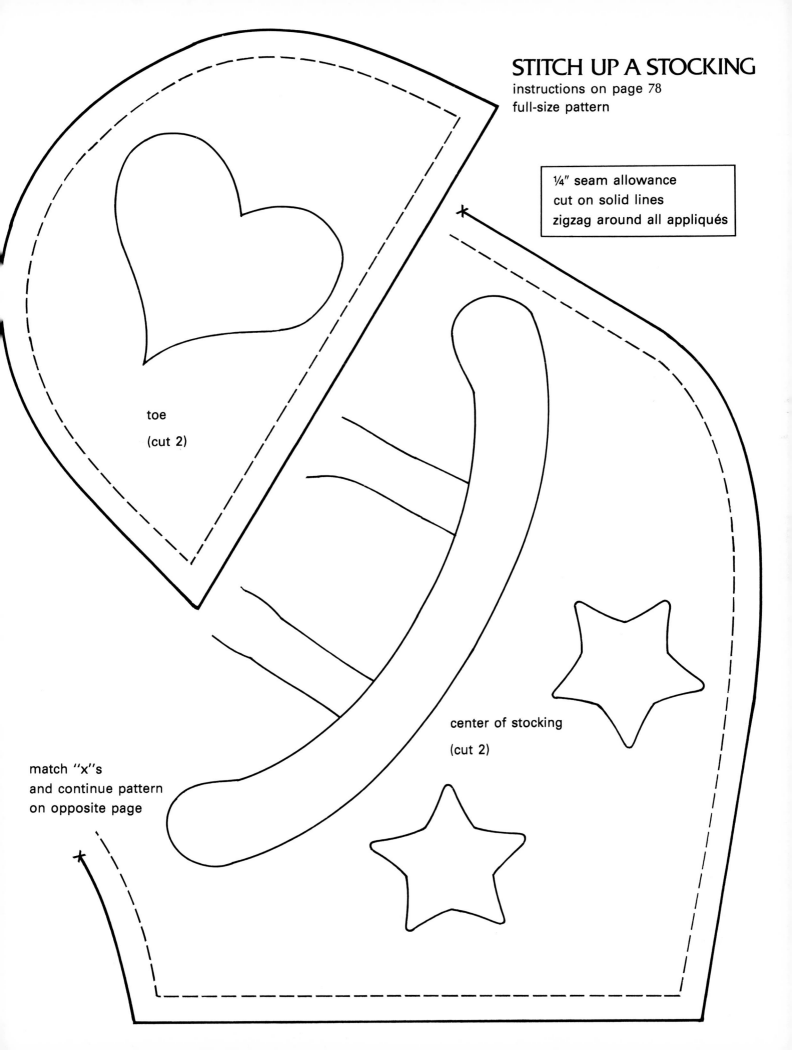

STITCH UP A STOCKING
instructions on page 78
full-size pattern

¼" seam allowance
cut on solid lines
zigzag around all appliqués

toe
(cut 2)

center of stocking
(cut 2)

match "x"s
and continue pattern
on opposite page

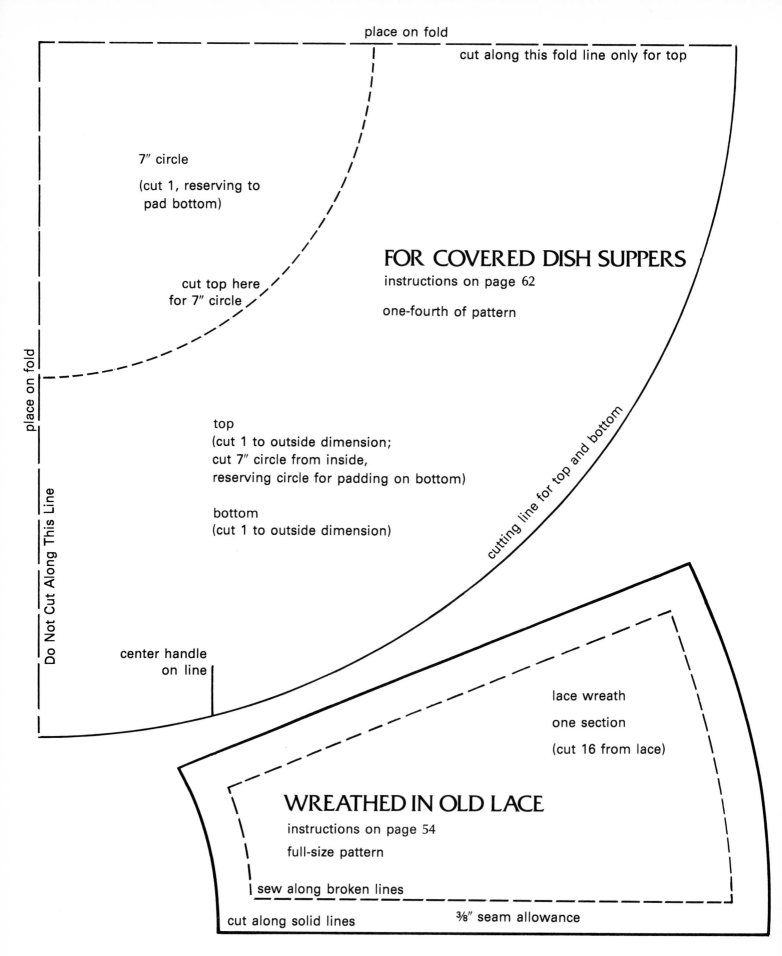

place on fold

cut along this fold line only for top

7" circle

(cut 1, reserving to pad bottom)

cut top here
for 7" circle

FOR COVERED DISH SUPPERS
instructions on page 62

one-fourth of pattern

place on fold

Do Not Cut Along This Line

top
(cut 1 to outside dimension;
cut 7" circle from inside,
reserving circle for padding on bottom)

bottom
(cut 1 to outside dimension)

cutting line for top and bottom

center handle
on line

lace wreath

one section

(cut 16 from lace)

WREATHED IN OLD LACE
instructions on page 54

full-size pattern

sew along broken lines

cut along solid lines   ⅜" seam allowance

144

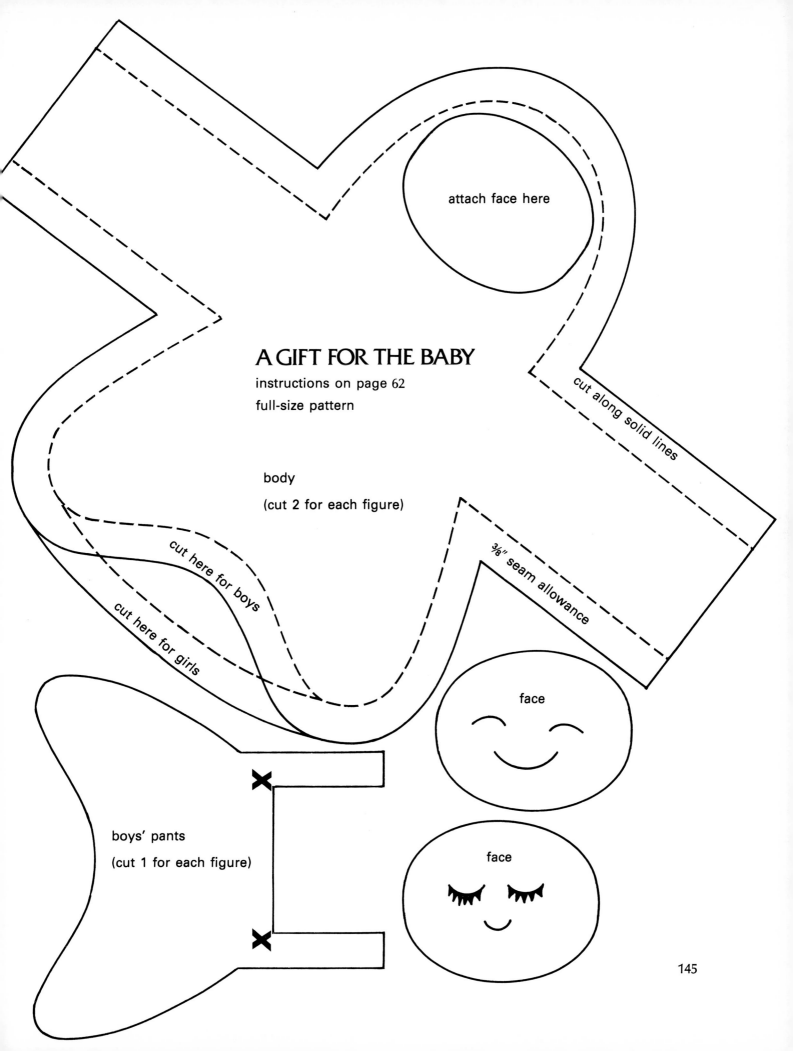

A GIFT FOR THE BABY

instructions on page 62

full-size pattern

attach face here

cut along solid lines

body

(cut 2 for each figure)

cut here for boys

cut here for girls

⅜" seam allowance

face

face

boys' pants

(cut 1 for each figure)

145

CARDS TO KEEP
instructions on page 88
full-size pattern

Color Key
(DMC Flosses)

- ◎ 961 dark dusty rose
- • 963 very light rose
- ◨ 503 med. blue green
- ◕ 816 garnet
- ☒ 437 light tan
- ○ 727 very light topaz
- ◲ 519 sky blue
- ◩ 435 very light brown
- ■ 3371 black brown
- ◿ white

Backstitch:

    around body 433 med. brown
    around ball on hat, scarf, and
       candleholder 435 very light brown
    around candle flame 816 garnet

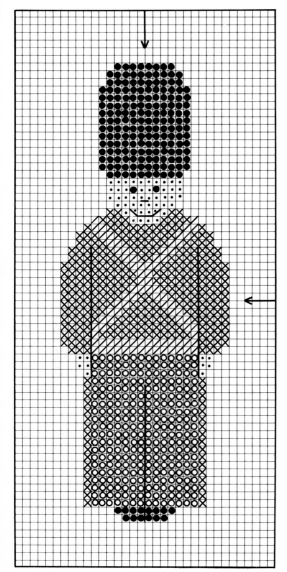

Backstitch with black
around arms, legs,
feet and mouth

146

Color Key
(DMC Flosses)

- ◎ 826 blue
- ☒ 666 red
- ◿ 725 gold
- ● 310 black
- • 353 flesh

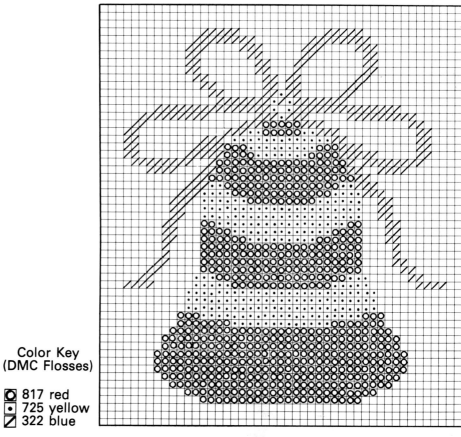

Color Key
(DMC Flosses)

- ◎ 817 red
- • 725 yellow
- ◿ 322 blue

backstitch around each color in bell with gold metallic

Color Key
(DMC Flosses)

⊠ 701 green
■ 699 dark green
◪ 666 red
◉ 498 dark red
⊡ 726 yellow
◐ 310 black

Backstitch with black

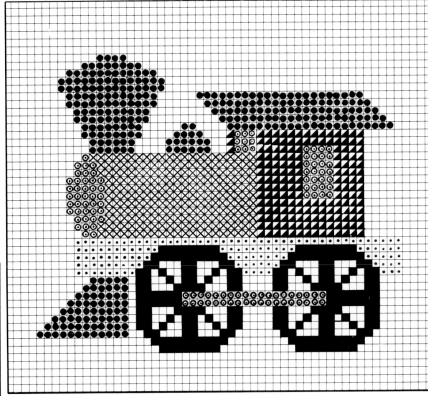

A TISKET, A TASKET

instructions on page 69
full-size pattern

Color Key
(DMC Flosses)

⊡ white
⊘ 415 gray
⊠ 741 orange
◉ 310 black
◪ 700 green
◉ 666 red
◣ 498 dark red

Backstitch with black around
each color and on edge of wing

A NEEDLEWORKER'S STOCKING

instructions on page 82

Color Key

- ◪ dark rose
- ⊠ med. rose
- ⊘ light rose
- ⧄ light blue
- − flesh
- ⊠ grey
- ◉ bright green
- ⋀ light green
- ⅄ dark rust
- ⋁ light rust
- ■ dark brown
- ◪ dark moss
- ◪ med. moss
- ◩ light moss
- ◉ bright red
- ● maroon
- ⦂ light yellow
- Ⅰ gold
- • cream

After marking outline on canvas (do not cut), work one row dark green continental stitch 2¼" below top of stocking. Center top row of clock (7 stitches wide) twelve vertical stitches below green row. Work design in continental and basketweave stitch. Chart initials. Center by placing center stitch of initials above center stitch of top row of clock and seven rows above line of green stitching. Fill in background with cream to outline of stocking.

Line up this arrow with the far left stitch of bottom row of rug (see chart on next page) with 17 vertical stitches between.

scale: 1 square equals 2" square

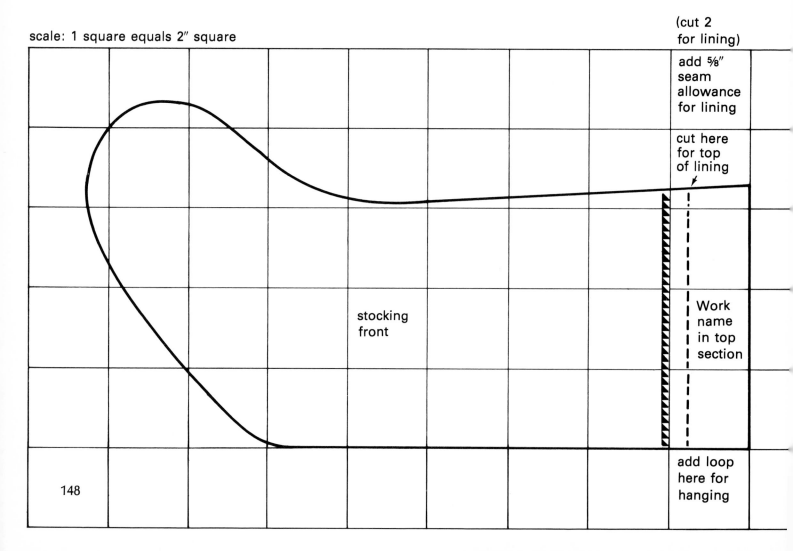

(cut 2 for lining)

add ⅝" seam allowance for lining

cut here for top of lining

Work name in top section

stocking front

148

add loop here for hanging

work background in white
make sewing thread by coming up
  from hoop and down at finger
make hands on clock in
  same manner

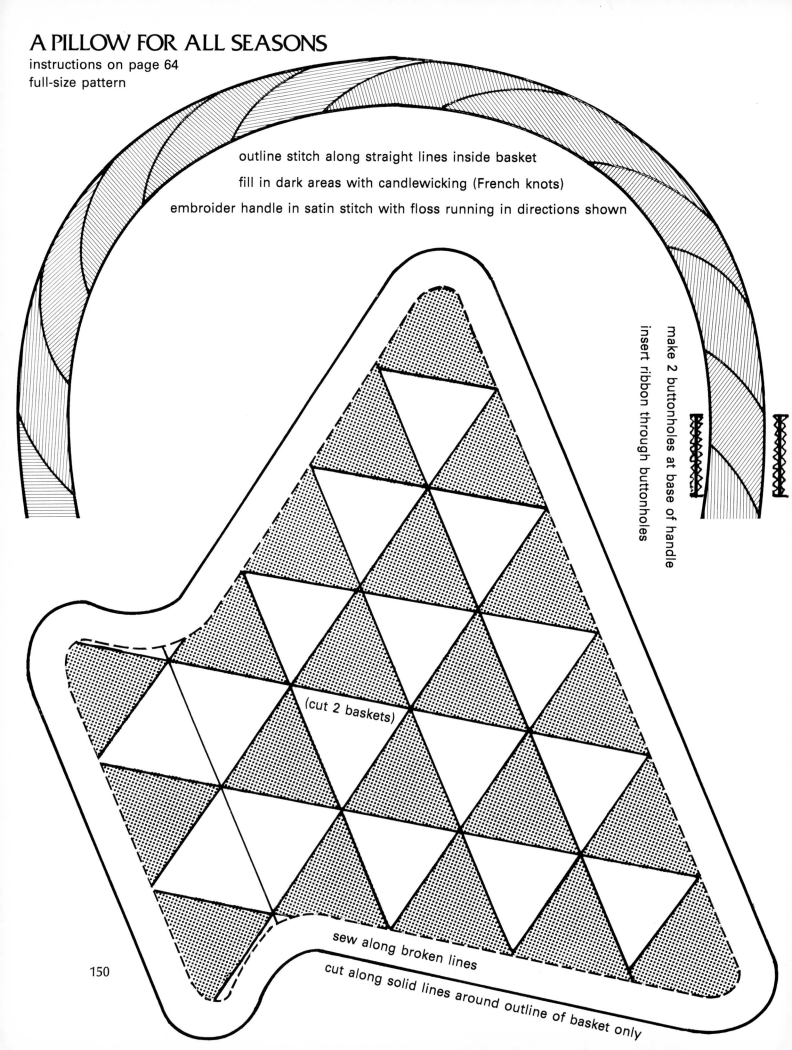

A PILLOW FOR ALL SEASONS

instructions on page 64
full-size pattern

outline stitch along straight lines inside basket

fill in dark areas with candlewicking (French knots)

embroider handle in satin stitch with floss running in directions shown

make 2 buttonholes at base of handle

insert ribbon through buttonholes

(cut 2 baskets)

sew along broken lines

cut along solid lines around outline of basket only

150

RECIPE INDEX

CONTRIBUTORS

Editorial Assistant: Pamela Hall
Production: Jerry Higdon, Jane Bonds, Jim Thomas
Design: Viola Andrycich
Cover Photograph: Beth Maynor
Art: Don K. Smith, Diana Smith, David Morrison
Art Director: Bob Nance

Special thanks to Susan Payne, Creative Foods Editor at *Decorating and Craft Ideas*, and to the Test Kitchens staff. Thanks also to the following people from *Southern Living*: Jean Wickstrom Liles, Foods Editor; Beverly Morrow, Foods Photo Stylist; and Vann Cleveland, Director of Photography.

DESIGNERS:

Jeffrey K. Adkisson, fruit and flower pyramid 8, chandelier with holly 38.

Diane C. Brakefield, bunny and goose boxes 52, ribbon-rose pincushion 54.

David B. Conard, log reindeer 28.

Inez Crimmins, ornaments on title page and 80, tree plaque 84.

Rita Bambi Martinez de Blake, St. Lucia Wreath 44

Anna Mary Duckworth, snowmen and trees on half-title page and 6, snowman box 7, gingerbread wreath 51 and 85, sleigh and skater ornaments 86 and 87.

Katie Dunn, pinecone door decoration on introduction page and 26.

Chris Emmert, peasant ornament 15.

Terry Fatout, reindeer stockings 78 and 79.

Jean Hafemann, memory cabinet 24, jewelled ornaments 90.

Beth Hamilton, ornaments 70 and 71.

Ann A. Harrison, peace banner 36.

Judy Hauenstein, knitted cap and ascot 58, crocheted animals 83.

Dora Hooks, elaeagnus wreath 32 and 33, cone and wheat wreath 43.

Maxine Hopping, sheep and shepherd 28.

Patricia J. Horton, candlewicked pillow 64, duck basket 69, needlepoint stocking 82, cross-stitch cards 88.

Donna B. Hunzinger, moose ornament 73.

Dottie Kent, chandelier with apples 38, decoys on chest 48.

Jo S. Kittinger, angel paper dolls 50.

Priscilla A. Lange, cone ornaments 23, cone in window 40, cone stickpin 59, shell ornament 65.

Sylvia S. Lindsley, Frère Jacques doll on cover and 56.

Susan Hoyt McCay, angel doll/treetopper 66, angel ornaments 68.

Freda McFarlane, reindeer riding toys 74-75.

Lorell Moore, vine goose, reindeer wreath, and nativity 34 and 35.

George F. Parr, mailbox with holly 36.

Diane Pelton, lamb ornament 72.

Michiko K. Petersen, crib kicker 62.

Teri Phillips, garland on staircase 30.

Frances Chadwick Reed, soft sculpture garland 76.

Suzanne Rippetoe, holiday slipcovers 21, fruits in window 39.

Ellis Ann Rodgers, mailbox with berries 36.

Edna Salyer, angel mantel on contents page and 22, nut tree 4, apple pyramid 9, exterior decorations 30 and 31, decoys on mantel 48, stacked boxes 49.

Jo Ann Salyers, bear collage 26.

Linda Schaefer, family tree ornament 88.

Shelley Stewart, table and chair covers, centerpiece 2 and 3; yo-yo jar toppers 10; bear ornaments 14; gift box centerpiece 16; sun ornaments and garland 20; candlestick mantel 22; button jars, candles in goblets, shells with lights 46 and 47; goody bags 77.

Carol M. Tipton, bear tree skirt 12.

Shirley Tipton, recipe holder 60.

Faye Toppen, casserole carrier 62.

Susan B. Tortoso, lace wreath 54.

Jo Voce, burlap bag ornaments 12, Mexican "God's-Eye" and yarn ornaments 18-20.

Carol L. Wagner, yo-yo wreath 10, snowflake quilt 40-42.

Martha Walthall and Linda Johnson, plaid placemats 16.

PHOTOGRAPHERS:

Katherine Adams, contents page, 5, 8, 9, 16, 21, top 22, 30, 31, 35, left 38, 39, top 46, top 48, top 49, 84.

Jim Bathie, 11, 43, 44, 53, 54, 63, 69, 70, 71.

Mike Clemmer, introduction, 26.

Frederica Georgia, 25, 28.

Mary-Gray Hunter, 17, 24, 33, bottom 46, 50, 60, 62, 64, 75, 76, 83, 89.

Bob Lancaster, right 7, 47.

Beth Maynor, cover, half-title page, title page, 1, 6, left 7, 15, 18, 20, 23, 27, right 38, bottom 48, bottom 49, 51, 55, 57, 61, 65, 68, 72, 73, 79, 81, 85, 86, 87, 88, 90.

John O'Hagan, 2, 3, 12, 13, 14, bottom 22, 29, 32, 34, 36, 37, 40, 41, 42, 58, 59, 66, 74, 78, 82, 95, 113, top 116.

Charles Walton, back cover, 77, 91, 93, 98, 103, 104, 107, 110, 115, bottom 116, 117, 118, 120.